This book is from
the kitchen library of

_____

ALSO BY ART GINSBURG, MR. FOOD®

The Mr. Food® Cookbook (1990)

Mr. Food® Cooks Like Mama (1992)

Mr. Food® Cooks Chicken (1993)

Mr. Food® Cooks Pasta (1993)

Mr. Food® Makes Dessert (1993)

Mr. Food® Cooks Real American (1994)

MR.FOOD®'S
Favorite
Cookies

Art Ginsburg
Mr. Food®

WILLIAM MORROW AND COMPANY, INC.

New York

Dedicated to
Ethel

It's so much easier for
two to climb than one

Library of Congress Cataloging-in-Publication Data

Ginsburg, Art.
    Mr. Food®'s favorite cookies / Art Ginsburg. — 1st ed.
      p. cm.
    Includes index.
    ISBN 0-688-13478-5
    1. Cookies. I. Title. II. Title: Mister Food's favorite
cookies.
    TX772.G56 1994
    641.8'654—dc20   94-21802
                                 CIP

Printed in the United States of America

First Edition

1 2 3 4 5 6 7 8 9 10

BOOK DESIGN BY MICHAEL MENDELSOHN/MM DESIGN 2000, INC.

ACKNOWLEDGMENTS

I can't figure out which I love more—the foods I write about or the people I write with!

Each book sure is easier to write than the last, mostly because of the great team I get to work with:

My daughter, Caryl Ginsburg Gershman, is still pulling it all together for me . . . beautifully! Howard Rosenthal has been a super new asset to the **MR. FOOD**® family and has provided incredible creativity to this particular project. A big thanks to my son Steve and to Roy Fantel for fine-tuning all the details.

As before, I gratefully acknowledge the creative input of Barbara Stevens and Carol Ginsburg, and also the baking talents of Linda Rose, Lori Puglisi, Jean Suits, and Maria Zemantauski.

And what a support staff! I couldn't do this without the conscientious assistance of Mary Ann Oliver, Marilyn Ruderman, Alice Palombo, Nancy Foraker, Grace Marshall, Madeline Burgan, and Loriann Bishop.

I truly appreciate the behind-the-scenes contributions of my agent, Bill Adler, my publicist, Phyllis Heller, and Al Marchioni, Harriet Bell, Skip Dye, Deborah Weiss Geline, and Bob Aulicino at William Morrow. Special thanks to all of you for your constant encouragement and enthusiasm.

I know that the work for this book was especially hard on my family and staff . . . it's rough having to constantly taste such awesome goodies! I thank my wife, Ethel, my son Chuck, my cookie-loving granddaughters, and everybody else for "sticking" around during all those gooey, chocolatey, definitely nutty recipe-testing days.

Probably the sweetest part about writing this book has been the reminder that I have so many warm and generous friends, viewers, and business associates. I thank all of you who've shared your scrumptious cookie favorites with me, especially:

Janice Acciardo

The American Dairy Board

Ann Baniak

Borden, Inc.

Rita Calvert

Millie Cohen

Pat Cooper

Anita Daly

Sharon Delles

Barbara Goldberg

Pat Higgins

Land O'Lakes, Inc.

McCormick®/Schilling®

Nestlé Food Corporation

The North Carolina Department of Agriculture

Debra Patterson

Teresa Pepe

Pillsbury

Chocolate Riesen® Caramels

Patty Rosenthal

SACO Foods, Inc., makers of Real Semisweet Chocolate Chunks

Alyce Scimeca

Granola Cookies recipe reprinted with the permission of General Mills, Inc.

HERSHEY'S, REESE'S, HUGS, and HUGS WITH ALMONDS are registered trademarks. Reese's Chewy Chocolate Cookies and Fudge Cheesecake Bars recipes courtesy of the Hershey Kitchens, and reprinted with permission of Hershey Foods Corporation.

Brown Sugar Brownies and Elfin Crispy Cake recipes courtesy of *Homemade Good News Magazine* and Savannah Foods & Industries, Inc., makers of Dixie Crystals Sugar.

Special thanks to Rawson, Inc., makers of fine cabinetry.

CONTENTS

INTRODUCTION

Mmm . . . Ahh . . .

Is it a dessert? A snack? A treat? A reward? It's all of those and more . . . it's a **COOKIE!**

Everybody loves cookies. In fact, there are more varieties of cookies than any other baked goods! Did you know that cookies as we know them today date back to the early colonial settlers of Dutch descent? They called their flat sweetened cakes *Koekje*, which translates to "little cake." *Cookie* is the American word.

Yes, there are so many types of cookies that it seems as if we could just keep on making different ones and never repeat. But we wouldn't do that, 'cause we'd never get back to our own special ones—the ones that make our mouths water, our knees wobble, and our hearts melt.

Sure, everyone's got 'em. From Vanilla Sugar Cookies (page 133) to Ultimate Chocolate Chunks (page 55), from Peanut Butter Oaties (page 43) to Double Chocolate Caramel Brownies (page 204), from Lemon Cheese Squares (page 178) to Hermits (page 171), we've all got our special crunchy, crispy, or chewy favorites.

When I was growing up, there was always some crunchy mandelbrot in our cookie jar. (As a kid I dunked it in ice cold milk; today I dunk it in my coffee.) It's the Eastern European version of Italian biscotti (like the Anise Biscuits on page 117), and it was there whether I wanted it for a snack, an after-dinner dessert, or even a breakfast dunker. And it was the same at my friends' houses, too—cookie jars full of tasty treasures—except that the favorite "regulars" were different at each house. I can remember them as if it were yesterday. Those orange cookies, poppy seed cookies, and special brownies were packed with flavor.

13

You know, it's really easy to fill our cookie jars today with those same tastes and textures. Why, I've got over 175 easy ways for you to make fun times and great memories for you and *your* family.

They're grouped into the usual cookie categories of drops, bars, shapes, icebox, and rolled cookies. Of course, I've added a few more chapters to help make you a real hero, like "No-Bake, No-Hassles," "Cookies by the Calendar," "Brownies, Everyone's Favorites," one filled with recipes for the kids to make along with you called "Fun Treats for Kids," and more! I've even added a final chapter full of dynamite drinks like "Steaming Mocha Cocoa" (page 242) and "Spicy Apple Cider" (page 245) called "To Wash It All Down."

Once again, I've collected recipes from my TV show as well as ones shared with me by viewers and old friends. They're quick and yummy, and you can probably make them with ingredients you already have on your shelves.

Before you get started, check out the charts and tips that follow. I've included lots of handy hints to help you with everything from properly measuring your ingredients to perfectly baking, storing, and even mailing your goodies. And at the beginning of each chapter I've included a bunch of really useful tips for making that specific type of cookie.

Oh—you'll notice that certain recipes throughout the book are marked with cookie jars. I call them my "Cookie Jar Favorites." It was tough to decide which ones to include, but these recipes are always overwhelming hits (*and* they can be stored in your cookie jar for easy access)! Look for those to be hands-down winners.

So, whether you like gooey chocolate, spicy gingerbread, zesty lemon, or even carrot or zucchini cookies, I know there'll be plenty of treats in here for you and your family and friends to make and enjoy together. Why, I wouldn't be surprised if you never *bought* cookies again!

Come on and get mixing, rolling, cutting, and baking . . . Tantalize those taste buds so your cookie jar, your tummies, and your mouths will be full of **OOH it's so GOOD!!**™

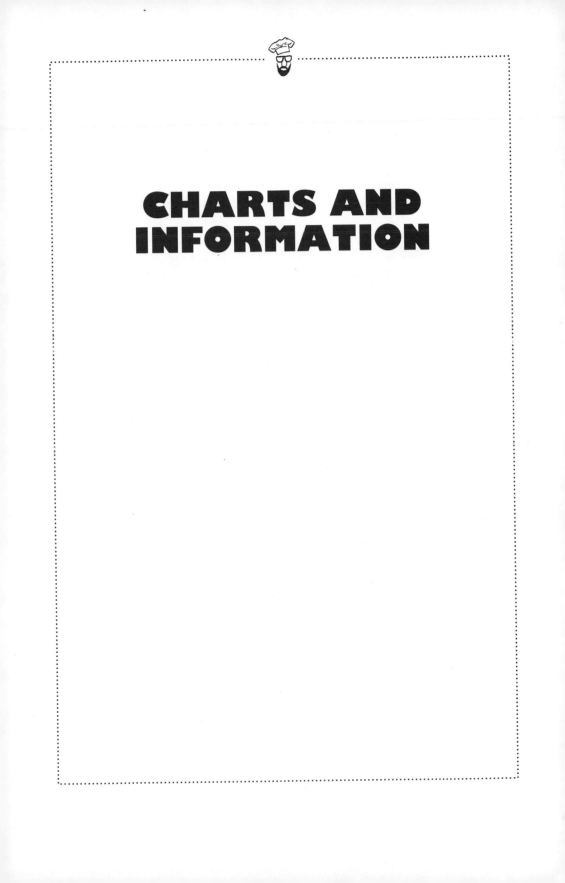

CHARTS AND INFORMATION

20 Tips for Making and Baking Great Cookies

Here are some general tips that apply to making and baking all cookies. Hints for the specific types of cookies are listed at the beginning of each chapter.

1. Always read a recipe completely before beginning, to be sure you understand the whole procedure. This will eliminate any surprises.
2. Gather all ingredients before beginning. Nobody wants to have to run to the store halfway through a recipe.
3. Unless specifically stated otherwise, ingredients are best when used at room temperature. This is true except in very hot kitchens.
4. The number of eggs called for in most recipes is based on U.S. graded large or extra-large eggs.
5. You can use butter or stick-type margarine unless otherwise instructed. Butter adds more flavor. If oversoftened, set it aside for other kitchen uses and use fresh for baking.
6. Mix dough evenly, making sure ingredients are combined uniformly. This is true except in recipes that state otherwise, such as marbleized items.
7. Overmixing can cause cookie dough to harden, so **do not overmix!**
8. To prevent the motor on your portable hand mixer from burning out, pay attention to how hard it is working. Cookie doughs tend to be stiff. You can almost always stir in your final dry ingredients by hand if necessary.
9. For best results, grease pans as directed in each recipe. This will ensure easy removal of cookies.
10. Always preheat the oven. Putting an item into a cold oven will alter the baking time and the consistency of the finished product.
11. To allow for the most even heat circulation, it is best to bake cookies and bars in the center oven rack position. Also, do not

overcrowd the oven. It will cause uneven baking, resulting in underbaked or burned cookies.

12. If baking two or more trays at the same time, it's best to place both pans into the oven at the same time, and switch the pan positions once during baking.

13. Never place raw cookie dough on a hot cookie sheet. If using the same cookie sheets for several batches, always allow them to cool between uses.

14. Always check cookies after the minimum suggested cooking time. Remember, cookies continue to bake after they're removed from the oven, so be careful not to overbake. A good rule of thumb is: Crispy, thin cookies are done if they're firm to the touch and golden around the edges. Thick or moist cookies are done when you can press them lightly with your finger and leave no imprint. Brownies and bars are done when they pull away slightly from the sides of the pan, or when firm to the touch with a little bounce (but not loose) when lightly pressed in the center.

15. Use a timer to help keep track of cooking time. It's easy to get distracted—and, if you do, your cookies can be overdone before you know it.

16. Always use pot holders or oven mitts when handling hot pans.

17. Place hot baking pans on a cooling rack to allow air to circulate completely around the pans. This also prevents damage to countertops.

18. If cooled cookies stick to a cookie sheet, return the pan to a warm oven for about 1 minute, then immediately remove the cookies with a spatula. The time needed will vary, depending on the oven temperature and specific cookies.

19. Test your oven temperature regularly with an oven thermometer to ensure proper calibration. Oven thermometers are usually available in supermarket housewares sections, and also in most kitchen stores.

20. Clean up as you go along so that your time in the kitchen can be enjoyable and kept to a minimum!

Charts and Information

What You Need to Make All Your Favorites

Baking cookies should be fun, easy, and hassle-free—a time to enjoy making those mouth-watering treats that the whole gang will love. But before we start, we need a few basic utensils to make our job even easier. These are all everyday household items—no fancy pans or gizmos. The following list should help.

- **Blender:** Helps speed up chopping or mixing of dry or liquid ingredients. Perfect for specialty drinks.

- **Cookie cutters:** Available in a variety of shapes and sizes, in both plastic and metal.

- **Cookie sheets:** For best results, select shiny metal or metal covered with a nonstick coating. Dark-surfaced sheets are also available but tend to bake faster. Baking times may vary with the weight and finish on each pan. Using insulated pans will result in an increased baking time. Have a few on hand since many recipes will require two or three pans to bake a single batch of cookies. The rimmed type is the most useful because it can be used for drop cookies as well as for most thin bar cookies. Be sure to check each recipe for the appropriate type and size of cookie sheet needed.

- **Cooling racks:** These allow air to circulate around the food after removing hot pans and cookie sheets from the oven. They help prevent burning countertops, too.

Charts and Information

- **Dry measuring cups:** Available in ¼-cup, ⅓-cup, ½-cup and 1-cup measurements for dry ingredients. Easy to level. Usually made of plastic or metal.

- **Electric mixer:** There are two basic varieties: the portable, hand-held type, ideal for cookies and lighter tasks, and the freestanding, tabletop type that's ideal for larger jobs and quantities.

- **Glass baking dishes:** Recommended for brownies and some bar cookies, they are oven-proof and available in standard sizes: 8" x 8", 9" x 9", 9" x 13", 10" x 13", and in 9" and 10" pie plates.

- **Glass measuring cups:** Most commonly available in 1-cup, 2-cup, and 4-cup sizes. Ideal for liquid measures.

- **Grater:** Perfect for lemon and orange peel (zest) and for grating cheese and chocolate.

- **Knives:** A sharp serrated (waved-edge) knife (like a bread knife) for cutting rolled cookies with firm mix-ins (raisins, nuts, etc.) and for cutting bars and brownies, too. A paring knife is just right for smaller jobs because it gives a greater feeling of control.

- **Measuring spoons:** Available in ¼-teaspoon, ½-teaspoon, 1-teaspoon, and 1-tablespoon measurements. Some sets also include ⅛-teaspoon. Usually made of plastic or metal and often connected on a ring for convenience.

- **Metal spatula or spreader:** A rounded-end knife with no cutting edge. Perfect for icing cookies and leveling off dry ingredients. Use for removing cookies, brownies, and bars from baking pans. Plastic spatulas are recommended when using nonstick pans to prevent scratching the surfaces.

- **Mixing bowls:** The basics of any kitchen. Usually graduated in size and made of stainless steel, glass, plastic, or earthenware. It's good to have at least one full set.

19

- **Mixing spoons:** You probably have a drawerful of wooden, plastic, or metal mixing spoons in a large variety of sizes. Unless a recipe specifies, the choice is yours.

- **Pot holders:** Available in mitten and pad types. A must for safe baking.

- **Rolling pin:** Wooden, metal, and marble rolling pins are available for rolling out dough. It is important to keep the surface clean and free from dents and nicks. When using, keep your rolling pin floured to prevent the dough from sticking.

- **Rubber spatula:** A helpful utensil for scraping down mixing bowls and for mixing ingredients. Sizes vary. Choose a strong one for mixing and a lighter one for icing and lighter jobs.

- **Ruler:** A plastic ruler is handy for measuring the diameter of rolled cookies or the thickness of roll-outs. Don't borrow the kids' ruler—keep one in the kitchen just for baking.

- **Saucepans:** An assortment of sizes are recommended. A double boiler (two pans that nest one over the other) is not necessary, but is often helpful.

- **Sifter:** Not a necessity but still helpful for removing lumps from flour and confectioners' sugar, and for mixing dry ingredients.

- **Timer:** A must for making cookie time worry-free time. Available as portable, digital, or built into your oven, in all shapes and sizes.

Common Baking Terms

Beat	To make a mixture smooth and introduce air by a brisk regular motion that lifts the mixture over and over. Usually done with an electric mixer.
Blend	To mix two or more ingredients so that each loses its individual identity. Done with an electric mixer, blender, or food processor.
Combine/ Mix	To join together two or more ingredients. Usually done by hand with a spoon.
Cream	To work foods, alone or with other ingredients, until soft and fluffy. Usually applied to shortening and sugar. Done by stirring, rubbing, or beating with a spoon or electric mixer.
Cut	To incorporate butter or solid shortening into dry ingredients with the least amount of blending, with the mixture ending up in small particles. Done by hand.
Fold in	To mix food gently, without releasing air bubbles. Usually done by hand, by scooping to the bottom center of the bowl via the side of the bowl and bringing bottom ingredients up over the top ingredients, until the foods are lightly combined. This method is done when it's necessary to keep individual ingredients intact, such as when adding nuts or chocolate morsels to a batter or when adding chocolate to whipped cream. It's also used to achieve a marbled effect.

21

| **Stir** | To use continuous movement to either combine ingredients, or to keep something from burning. Usually done by hand. |
| **Whip** | To beat into a froth, as with eggs or cream. Usually done with an electric mixer. |

Measuring Tips

Proper measuring is key to good cookie baking, and it's easy to get it right if you follow a few basic rules:

- **Measuring liquids:** Use a clear glass or plastic measuring cup with a pouring spout. They're marked in varying increments from ¼ cup to 1 cup and up, depending on the size chosen. Make certain you have the cup on a level surface and read it at eye level for an accurate reading.

- **Measuring dry ingredients:** Fill dry measuring cups with dry ingredients and level with a knife or spatula to even off the top of the cup. Sizes are ¼ cup, ⅓ cup, ½ cup, 1 cup, and 2 cups.

- **Measuring spoons:** These are for measuring small amounts of wet or dry ingredients. Use dry by filling up the spoon and leveling it off with a knife or spatula. Liquid ingredients are measured by pouring a liquid into the spoon until it is full and level.

- **Measuring butter:** Measurable amounts are printed on most stick butter wrappers. Follow the guidelines on page 23 for quick and easy measuring.

⅛ stick = 1 tablespoon = ½ ounce
¼ stick = 2 tablespoons = 1 ounce
½ stick = 4 tablespoons = 2 ounces
1 stick = ½ cup = 4 ounces
2 sticks = 1 cup = 8 ounces
4 sticks = 2 cups = 16 ounces

Weights and Measures

EQUALS

Dash	less than ⅛ teaspoon
3 teaspoons	1 tablespoon
4 tablespoons	¼ cup
5 tablespoons plus 1 teaspoon	⅓ cup
8 tablespoons	½ cup
10 tablespoons plus 2 teaspoons	⅔ cup
12 tablespoons	¾ cup
16 tablespoons	1 cup
2 tablespoons	1 fluid ounce
1 cup	½ pint or 8 fluid ounces
2 cups	1 pint or 16 fluid ounces
4 cups	2 pints or 1 quart or 32 fluid ounces
4 quarts	1 gallon or 128 fluid ounces
Juice of 1 lemon	about 3 tablespoons
Juice of 1 orange	about ½ cup
Grated peel of 1 lemon	about 1½ teaspoons
Grated peel of 1 orange	about 1 tablespoon

Charts and Information

I POUND* OF	EQUALS APPROXIMATELY
Flour	4 cups
Sugar	2 cups
Brown sugar	3 cups
Confectioners' sugar	3½ cups
Raisins	3 cups

*One pound equals 16 ounces avoirdupois (our usual standard of weight measurement).

Ingredient Substitutions

These substitutions will work in most recipes, but results may vary with specific recipes, so go ahead and experiment!

EQUALS

I tablespoon cornstarch	2 tablespoons flour *or* 1⅓ tablespoons minute tapoica
I cup corn syrup	I cup granulated sugar plus ¼ cup water
I cup honey	1¼ cups granulated sugar plus ¼ cup water
I ounce chocolate	I square of baker's chocolate *or* ¼ cup cocoa plus ½ tablespoon shortening
I cup milk	½ cup evaporated milk plus ½ cup water *or* ⅓ cup nonfat dry milk plus water to make I cup
I teaspoon baking powder	¼ teaspoon baking soda plus ½ teaspoon cream of tartar *or* ¼ teaspoon baking soda plus ½ cup fully soured milk *or* ¼ teaspoon baking soda plus ¼ to ½ cup molasses

1 cup sour cream	3 tablespoons melted butter stirred into buttermilk or yogurt to make 1 cup
1 cup heavy cream	⅓ cup melted butter plus ¾ cup milk
Ricotta cheese	Cottage cheese, liquid drained

Tips for Reducing Fat and Calories in Homemade Cookies

These substitutions will work in most recipes, but results may vary with specific recipes, so go ahead and experiment!

- Use low-fat or skim milk in place of whole milk.

- Experiment with using low-fat or fat-free sour cream and yogurt in place of traditional sour cream and yogurt.

- Many recipes will still work if you substitute fruit juice for milk and cut down slightly on the amount of sugar in the recipe. Try it with your favorite recipes. Each recipe will react differently, but maybe you'll come up with some new favorites! (Unfortunately, the ones in the chapter "To Wash It All Down" *won't* work if you do that.)

- Try using frozen or refrigerated egg substitute in place of whole fresh eggs to reduce calories, fat, and cholesterol. Read the package for specific equivalency.

- Cut back on the amount of chocolate chips, nuts, raisins, and other end-of-recipe "add-ins." This will usually cut back on your fat and calorie intake without sacrificing too much flavor.

Storage of Cookies

There's nothing better than a cookie fresh from the oven. Usually they're eaten as fast as we can bake them! But if there are any left, it's important to store them properly so they retain their freshness. After all, no one wants a cookie that tastes old or dry.

- Be sure to cool cookies completely before packing them in containers or cookie jars.

- Don't store chewy cookies with brittle cookies; store them separately.

- Do not stack iced cookies unless you separate each layer with parchment or waxed paper.

- Most cookies can be stored for up to one week at room temperature or, if wrapped tightly, up to four months in the freezer.

- In general, thaw frozen cookies at room temperature for 30 minutes before serving.

- To maintain a fresher taste, freeze brownies and bar cookies whole (uncut).

- If planning to freeze frosted or iced cookies, frost or ice them *after* freezing, not before, to prevent smearing.

Mailing Cookies

One of the best parts of making cookies is sharing them with family and friends. It's certainly easy enough to bring a platter of cookies over to your neighbor's house. For those longer journeys, however, you need to

26

know a few tricks. Here are some tips to help ship cookies so that the folks at the receiving end will enjoy them as fresh-tasting and good-looking as when you made them.

- Round cookies travel best. Cookies that have points are more apt to break during travel. Avoid sending shortbread-type cookies if possible, since they're brittle. Avoid shipping cookies that have delicate icings and decorations that may smear or smudge during travel.

- Bars and brownies travel well, as do moist cookies. If shipping both crisp and moist cookies, wrap them separately so that each retains its own texture.

- For easier packing, wrap cookies in small bunches, rather than in one large bundle.

- Pack bunches of cookies in a sturdy box, cookie tin, or large coffee can to help them retain their shape and freshness.

- Place heavy cookies on the bottom of the package and lighter cookies on the top.

- Wrap cookies snugly in the package to avoid excessive movement.

- Choose an appropriate cushion for packaging, such as paper towels, waxed paper, shredded paper, or popcorn (popped and unbuttered). I recommend enclosing a note saying to discard the popcorn after unpacking, since it was used for shipping purposes only.

- It's better to send several smaller packages (five pounds or under), rather than one large package of goodies.

- Seal the package with adhesive or freezer tape. Wrap the outside of each package with plain heavy mailing tape or a brown grocery bag.

- Print mailing address and return address clearly with a permanent ink pen or marker so it won't smear if it gets wet.

- For prompt delivery, mark the package "Perishable—Food" and mark the top "This Side Up."

- Check with your local carrier as to the quickest, safest recommended shipping method for your package.

Packaged Foods Note

As with many processed foods, package sizes may vary by brand. Generally, the sizes indicated in these recipes are average sizes. If you can't find the exact indicated package size, whatever package is closest in size will usually do the trick.

Drop by Drop

Boy, oh boy, do I like making drop cookies! I think they're special to me 'cause my first memories are of Grandma baking these always-so-good cookies in no time.

We call them drop cookies because that's exactly how we make 'em. The dough is usually softer than the dough for rolled or icebox cookies, and it can be mixed either by hand with a wooden spoon or with an electric beater. You have lots of fun add-ins to choose from, like chocolate chips, fruit, candies, or even pieces of other cookies. The dough is then dropped by heaping teaspoons (dinnerware, not measuring spoons) onto either a greased or ungreased cookie sheet—whatever the recipe calls for. Don't worry if you make them large one time and a little smaller the next, because these cookies are very cooperative, with perfect or near-perfect results every time. Just make sure that the cookies on each sheet are dropped the same size so that they bake evenly. The baking time may vary slightly because of variations in oven temperature, dough thickness, cookie size, and the type of cookie sheet you use. So, roll up your sleeves and get ready to fill your cookie jars—simply and scrumptiously.

Tips

- Use two dinnerware teaspoons to drop the cookies: one to scoop up the dough and the other to help transfer the dough to a cookie sheet. Some professionals prefer using a tiny ice cream scoop to make sure each cookie is the same size.

- Space cookies evenly on the cookie sheets. Try baking just one or two cookies first to see how far they spread before using all the dough. This will prevent the cookies from baking together.

- Never put raw dough on a hot cookie sheet because the cookies will bake unevenly and spread out.

- Remember, cookies continue baking for a few minutes after removal from the oven, so do not overbake them by leaving them in the oven too long.

- Drop cookies are usually done when the bottoms and edges are golden brown.

Drop by Drop

Cookie Jar Favorites

Cookie Jar Favorites

Drop by Drop

Incredible Chocolate Chunks

about 4 dozen cookies

There's no better place to start—every bite is ecstasy! The name sure fits. These are absolutely **INCREDIBLE!**

1½ cups rolled oats
2 cups all-purpose flour
½ teaspoon baking powder
1 teaspoon baking soda
½ teaspoon salt
1 cup (2 sticks) butter, softened
1 cup granulated sugar

1 cup light brown sugar
1 tablespoon vanilla extract
2 eggs
2 cups (1 12-ounce package) semisweet chocolate chunks
1½ cups chopped walnuts

Preheat the oven to 375°F. Place the oats in a blender or food processor and crush to a fine powder on highest setting. Place the powdered oats in a medium-sized bowl and add the flour, baking powder, baking soda, and salt. In a large bowl, combine the butter, sugars, and vanilla; beat until creamy. Beat in the eggs. Gradually add the oat mixture. Stir in the chocolate chunks and the walnuts. Drop by heaping teaspoonfuls onto greased cookie sheets. Bake for 10 to 12 minutes. Cool on wire racks.

Drop by Drop

Fresh Apple Cookies

about 4 dozen cookies

Have a few extra apples left over? Are they starting to get soft? Here's a great way to use them up and still bring fresh orchard taste to each and every cookie.

½ cup vegetable shortening
1⅓ cups firmly packed brown sugar
½ teaspoon salt
1 teaspoon ground cinnamon
1 teaspoon ground nutmeg
1 egg

2 cups all-purpose flour
1 teaspoon baking soda
¼ cup milk
2 cups peeled, cored, and finely chopped apples, any variety
1 cup chopped walnuts

Vanilla Glaze

1½ cups confectioners' sugar
1 tablespoon butter, melted

½ teaspoon vanilla extract
⅛ teaspoon salt
3 tablespoons milk

Preheat the oven to 400°F. In a large bowl, cream the shortening, brown sugar, salt, cinnamon, nutmeg, and egg. Add the flour and baking soda, mixing well. Stir in the milk until well blended. Stir in the apples and nuts. Drop by teaspoonfuls onto cookie sheets that have been coated with nonstick vegetable cooking spray. Bake for 11 to 14 minutes or until golden. While baking, in a small bowl, combine all the glaze ingredients and mix to a smooth consistency. Remove cookies from the cookie sheets and, while still hot, spread with the vanilla glaze.

NOTE: Cool before storing so the cookies won't stick to each other.

Drop by Drop

Oatmeal Raisin Drops

about 2½ dozen cookies

These are simply down-home delicious and easy as can be.

1 cup (2 sticks) butter, softened
1 cup granulated sugar
½ cup firmly packed brown sugar
2 eggs

1 teaspoon vanilla extract
2 cups all-purpose flour
1 teaspoon salt
1 teaspoon baking soda
1½ cups rolled oats
1¼ cups raisins

Preheat the oven to 375°F. In a large bowl, cream together the butter, sugars, eggs, and vanilla. Stir in the flour, salt, baking soda, and oats; mix well. Stir in the raisins. Drop by tablespoonfuls onto lightly greased cookie sheets. Bake for 10 to 12 minutes or until lightly browned. Remove to wire racks to cool.

Drop by Drop

Doubly Chocolate Chewies

2½ to 3 dozen cookies

What could possibly be better than a chocolate cookie, except a chocolate cookie with twice the chocolate?!

1 cup (2 sticks) butter,
   softened
1½ cups sugar
2 eggs
2 teaspoons vanilla extract
2 cups all-purpose flour
⅔ cup baking cocoa

¾ teaspoon baking soda
¼ teaspoon salt
1 package (12 ounces)
   semisweet chocolate chips
½ cup chopped walnuts
   (optional)

Preheat the oven to 350°F. In a large bowl, beat the butter, sugar, eggs, and vanilla until light and fluffy. In another large bowl, combine the flour, cocoa, baking soda, and salt; add to the butter mixture. Stir in the chocolate chips and nuts. Drop by teaspoonfuls onto ungreased cookie sheets. Bake for 8 to 10 minutes or just until set. Cool slightly before removing from the cookie sheets.

Grandma's Spice Cookies

4 to 5 dozen cookies

Yesterday's old-fashioned taste with today's convenient ingredients.

- 1 package (18.5 ounces) spice cake mix
- 1 cup (2 sticks) butter, softened
- 2 eggs
- 1 cup flaked coconut
- 1 cup chopped walnuts
- 1 cup crushed corn flakes
- 1 cup rolled oats
- 1 cup raisins
- 2 tablespoons sugar

Preheat the oven to 350°F. In a large bowl, combine the cake mix, butter, and eggs; mix well. Add the coconut, walnuts, corn flakes, rolled oats, and raisins; mix well. Drop the dough by rounded teaspoonfuls 2 inches apart onto ungreased cookie sheets. Flatten them with a glass that's repeatedly dipped in the sugar. Bake for 8 to 12 minutes or until set. Cool for 1 minute, then remove from cookie sheets and let cool.

NOTE: To crush corn flakes, place them in a plastic bag and crush with a rolling pin.

Drop by Drop

Italian Dippers

about 2½ dozen cookies

Nothing is better than anise cookies dipped into a mug of steaming hot chocolate.

4 eggs	⅛ teaspoon salt
1 cup sugar	2 cups all-purpose flour
1¼ tablespoons anise extract	2 teaspoons baking powder

Preheat the oven to 350°F. In a large bowl, cream the eggs and sugar until creamy. Add the anise extract. Slowly beat the salt, flour, and baking powder into the egg mixture until smooth and creamy. Drop the batter by teaspoonfuls about 2 inches apart, in oblong shapes, onto cookie sheets that have been buttered and lightly sprinkled with flour. Bake for 10 to 12 minutes or until golden.

Zucchini Cookies

about 4 dozen cookies

Zucchini for dessert?! We've been enjoying zucchini in bread for many years . . . now here's another sweet way to enjoy it!

½ cup (1 stick) butter,
   softened
1 cup sugar
1 egg, beaten
2 cups all-purpose flour
1 teaspoon baking soda
1 teaspoon ground cinnamon

½ teaspoon salt
1 cup grated zucchini (about
   1 small zucchini)
1 cup raisins
1 cup chopped walnuts
1 cup (1 6-ounce package)
   semisweet chocolate chips

Preheat the oven to 350°F. In a large bowl, cream together the butter and sugar until light and fluffy. Gradually add the egg, flour, baking soda, cinnamon, and salt; mix well. Stir in the zucchini, raisins, walnuts, and chocolate chips. Drop by teaspoonfuls onto cookie sheets that have been coated with nonstick vegetable cooking spray. Bake for 15 to 20 minutes or until golden. Do not overbake.

Drop by Drop

Reese's Chewy Chocolate Cookies

about 4½ dozen cookies

Don't make these cookies if you're going to want your company to leave early . . . they'll want to stay until they're all eaten up!

2 cups all-purpose flour
¾ cup Hershey's cocoa
1 teaspoon baking soda
½ teaspoon salt
1¼ cups (2½ sticks) butter, softened

2 cups sugar
2 eggs
2 teaspoons vanilla extract
1⅔ cups (1 10-ounce package) Reese's Peanut Butter Chips

Preheat the oven to 350°F. In a large bowl, combine the flour, cocoa, baking soda, and salt. In another large bowl, beat the butter and sugar until light and fluffy. Add the eggs and vanilla; beat well. Gradually add the flour mixture, beating well. Stir in the peanut butter chips. Drop by rounded teaspoonfuls onto ungreased cookie sheets. Bake for 8 to 9 minutes. Cool slightly, then remove cookies to a wire rack to cool completely.

NOTE: Do not overbake these—they should be soft. They'll puff while baking and flatten while cooling.

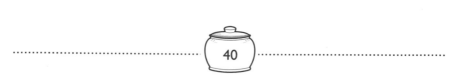

Drop by Drop

Sour Cream Cookies

about 2½ dozen cookies

My sister always wins rave reviews when she makes these for her bridge club.

1 cup firmly packed brown sugar	2 teaspoons baking powder
½ cup (1 stick) butter, softened	½ teaspoon baking soda
	½ teaspoon salt
1 egg	1 teaspoon ground cinnamon
2 cups all-purpose flour	½ cup sour cream
	1 cup chopped walnuts

Preheat the oven to 400°F. In a large bowl, cream together the brown sugar and butter until light and creamy. Add the egg, mixing well. In a medium-sized bowl, combine the flour, baking powder, baking soda, salt, and cinnamon. Alternately add the flour mixture and the sour cream to the butter mixture. Mix well, then stir in the nuts. Drop by heaping teaspoonfuls 2 inches apart on a cookie sheet that has been coated with nonstick vegetable cooking spray. Bake for 10 to 12 minutes or until no imprint is left when cookies are pressed lightly. Immediately remove to a wire rack to cool.

NOTE: Low-fat sour cream will work just as well as regular in these.

Molasses Ginger Rounds

about 3 dozen cookies

A traditional favorite with an orange "twist."

2 cups all-purpose flour
1 teaspoon baking soda
½ teaspoon salt
1½ teaspoons ground nutmeg
1½ teaspoons ground ginger
1½ teaspoons ground
   cinnamon

⅓ cup butter, softened
½ cup granulated sugar
1 egg
½ cup molasses
⅓ cup boiling water
2 cups seedless raisins

Creamy Orange Icing

2 cups confectioners' sugar
1 teaspoon vanilla extract
2 tablespoons butter,
   softened

1 teaspoon grated orange rind
2 to 3 tablespoons orange
   juice

In a medium-sized bowl, sift together the flour, baking soda, salt, nutmeg, ginger, and cinnamon. In a large bowl, cream the ⅓ cup butter, gradually adding the granulated sugar and creaming well. Blend in the egg, then add the dry ingredients alternately with the molasses and boiling water, mixing well. Stir in the raisins. Cover and chill for 45 to 60 minutes. Preheat the oven to 350°F. Drop by rounded teaspoonfuls onto cookie sheets that have been lightly coated with nonstick vegetable cooking spray. Bake for 8 to 10 minutes. Meanwhile, place the confectioners' sugar, vanilla, 2 tablespoons butter, and orange rind in a large bowl. Gradually blend in the orange juice until the icing is of spreading consistency. Top the warm cookies with the icing.

NOTE: These are lip smackin' delicious even without the icing.

Drop by Drop

Peanut Butter Oaties

about 5 dozen cookies

You can bet all the kids (yes, the big ones, too!) will be wild for these.

1¼ cups all-purpose flour
1 teaspoon baking powder
1 teaspoon baking soda
¼ teaspoon salt
2½ cups quick-cooking oats
1 cup (2 sticks) butter

1 cup peanut butter
1 cup granulated sugar
1 cup firmly packed brown
   sugar
2 eggs
1 teaspoon vanilla extract

Preheat the oven to 350°F. In a large bowl, combine the flour, baking powder, baking soda, salt, and oats; set aside. In a small saucepan, melt the butter over low heat; add the peanut butter and heat, stirring, until smooth. In another large bowl, combine the sugars, eggs, and vanilla; add the peanut butter mixture and blend thoroughly. Gradually add the flour mixture, blending well by hand. Drop by teaspoonfuls onto ungreased cookie sheets. Bake for 12 to 15 minutes or until golden. Remove from cookie sheets and cool.

NOTE: If you'd like a little variety, stir in some chopped walnuts and/ or raisins after the dough is well blended.

Chocolate Potato Cookies

about 4½ dozen cookies

Mashed potatoes in a cookie?? Unbelievable?? Sshh, let's keep this our secret!

1 cup firmly packed brown sugar
½ cup vegetable shortening
1 egg
1 teaspoon almond extract
½ cup semisweet chocolate chips, melted
½ cup unseasoned mashed potatoes, at room temperature

1½ cups all-purpose flour
½ teaspoon salt
½ teaspoon baking soda
¾ cup milk
½ cup chopped walnuts or pecans
1 can (16 ounces) chocolate fudge frosting
¼ cup nonpareils

Preheat the oven to 400°F. In a large bowl, cream together the brown sugar and shortening until light and fluffy. Beat in the egg and almond extract, mixing well. Add the melted chocolate and the mashed potatoes, beating until smooth. In a small bowl, combine the flour, salt, and baking soda. Alternately add the flour mixture and the milk to the shortening mixture, stirring until smooth. Mix in the nuts. Drop by rounded teaspoonfuls 2 inches apart onto cookie sheets that have been coated with nonstick vegetable cooking spray. Bake for 10 minutes or until cookies spring back when touched lightly with a finger. Remove from the oven and let cookies remain on baking sheet for a minute or two before removing to a wire rack to cool. Frost the warm cookies and sprinkle with the nonpareils.

NOTE: You should use only real mashed potatoes in this recipe.

Banana Cherry Cookies

about 7 dozen cookies

There's no need to monkey around with this yummy recipe . . .

1 cup vegetable shortening
1½ cups sugar
2 eggs
1 teaspoon vanilla extract
2¾ cups all-purpose flour
1½ teaspoons baking soda
½ teaspoon salt

½ cup buttermilk
1 cup mashed ripe bananas
  (about 3 medium-sized
  bananas)
1 cup chopped walnuts
½ cup chopped candied
  cherries

Preheat the oven to 375°F. Cream the shortening and sugar in a large bowl until light and fluffy. Add the eggs and vanilla; blend well. In another large bowl, combine the flour, baking soda, and salt. Alternately add the flour mixture, the buttermilk, and the mashed bananas to the shortening mixture. Stir in the nuts and candied cherries. (The dough will be soft.) Drop by teaspoonfuls onto cookie sheets that have been coated with nonstick vegetable cooking spray. Bake for 8 to 10 minutes or until golden. Cool slightly, then remove the cookies to a wire rack to cool completely.

NOTE: Here's a great way to use up those bananas that are a bit too ripe.

Cookie Jar Favorite

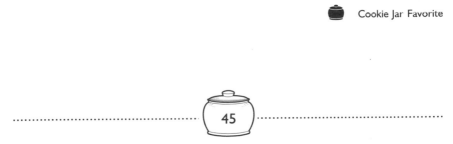

Mocha Snowcaps

about 3 dozen cookies

Looking for something different? Something rich? Something chewy? Here they are!

2 cups all-purpose flour
½ teaspoon salt
½ teaspoon baking soda
3 squares (1 ounce each)
    unsweetened baking
    chocolate
¼ cup hot coffee

½ cup (1 stick) butter
1 cup firmly packed brown
    sugar
1 egg
½ cup sour cream
1 cup flaked coconut, divided

Chocolate Frosting

1 square (1 ounce)
    unsweetened baking
    chocolate

1 tablespoon unsalted butter
2 tablespoons sour cream
1 cup confectioners' sugar

Preheat the oven to 375°F. In a small bowl, combine the flour, salt, and baking soda; set aside. In a small saucepan, melt the chocolate in the coffee over low heat; set aside to cool. In a large bowl, cream together the butter and brown sugar. Add the egg and the cooled chocolate mixture and beat well. Add the sour cream and the flour mixture alternately, mixing well. Add ½ cup of the coconut and mix well. Drop by heaping teaspoonfuls onto greased cookie sheets. Bake for 12 to 15 minutes. Meanwhile, in a small microwaveable bowl, melt the chocolate, butter, and sour cream on low power in the microwave. Mix well, then slowly blend in the confectioners' sugar and mix again. Frost cookies while warm and sprinkle tops with the remaining coconut.

NOTE: If the consistency of the frosting seems too thick, mix in a few drops of heavy cream or water.

Drop by Drop

Cooked Carrot Cookies

about 3 dozen cookies

What an easy way to get your kids to eat carrots. They'll never know!

1 cup granulated sugar
½ cup vegetable shortening
1 cup mashed cooked carrots
   (see Note)
1 egg
1 teaspoon vanilla extract

2 cups all-purpose flour
¼ teaspoon salt
2 teaspoons baking powder
2 tablespoons grated orange
   peel

Glaze

4 tablespoons confectioners'
   sugar

1 tablespoon orange juice

Preheat the oven to 350°F. In a large bowl, cream the granulated sugar and shortening until light and fluffy. Add the carrots, egg, and vanilla, beating until well blended. Beat in the flour, salt, baking powder, and orange peel until blended. Drop by teaspoonfuls 2 inches apart on a cookie sheet that has been coated with nonstick vegetable cooking spray. Bake for 18 to 20 minutes or until golden. While baking, combine the glaze ingredients in a small bowl and mix until smooth. Cool the cookies slightly, then remove to a wire rack to cool completely. When cool, distribute evenly with the glaze.

NOTE: You can mash fresh-cooked carrots or canned carrots for this recipe. It works with either! (1 cup mashed = 3 to 4 medium-sized fresh-cooked carrots or about 1 16-ounce can of carrots, drained)

Banana Bread Bites

about 6 dozen

Here's the homemade taste of banana bread with the ease of cookies. What a treat!

1 cup sugar	½ teaspoon salt
½ cup vegetable shortening	1 cup mashed bananas
2 eggs	(about 3 ripe bananas)
1 teaspoon baking soda	1 teaspoon vanilla extract
2 cups all-purpose flour	½ cup chopped walnuts

Preheat the oven to 350°F. In a large bowl, cream together the sugar and shortening until light and fluffy. Add the eggs and beat thoroughly. Gradually blend in the baking soda, flour, and salt. Beat in the mashed bananas and vanilla until well mixed. Fold in the chopped walnuts. Drop the mixture by teaspoonfuls onto cookie sheets that have been coated with nonstick vegetable cooking spray. Bake for 12 to 15 minutes or until light golden. Remove from cookie sheets immediately and place on a wire rack to cool.

NOTE: If you like these a bit sweeter, as I do, use an additional ¼ cup sugar.

Drop by Drop

Chocolate Chocolate Chunks

about 2 dozen

Hoo boy, a rich-tasting chocolate cookie that's quick and simple to make. Will they love 'em? You bet!

1 ¾ cups all-purpose flour
¼ teaspoon baking soda
1 cup (2 sticks) butter, softened
1 cup granulated sugar
½ cup light brown sugar
1 teaspoon vanilla extract
⅓ cup baking cocoa

2 tablespoons light cream
2 cups (1 12-ounce package) semisweet chocolate chunks
1 cup chopped pecans (optional)

Preheat the oven to 350°F. In a large bowl, combine the flour and baking soda; set aside. In another large bowl, with an electric mixer, cream together the butter and sugars; add the vanilla and mix well. Add the cocoa and beat until well blended. Add the cream and, on low speed, gradually add the flour mixture; beat until mixed. Stir in the chocolate chunks and nuts, if using. Drop by heaping tablespoonfuls onto greased cookie sheets; flatten the cookies slightly. Bake for 12 to 13 minutes. Do not overbake (the cookies should feel soft when done.) Cool for 2 minutes on the cookie sheets, then remove to wire racks to cool completely.

Cookie Jar Favorite

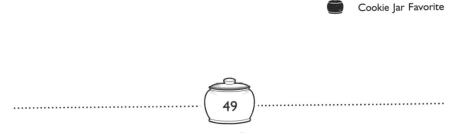

Drop by Drop

Maple Walnut Drops

about 2 dozen

Boy, oh boy, I really love the taste of real maple syrup. And these are like taking a trip to Vermont with every bite.

½ cup (1 stick) butter, softened
¼ cup firmly packed brown sugar
¼ cup granulated sugar
2 tablespoons maple syrup

1 teaspoon vanilla extract
¾ cup all-purpose flour
½ cup rolled oats
¼ teaspoon salt
½ cup finely chopped walnuts

Preheat the oven to 350°F. In a medium-sized bowl, beat the butter, sugars, maple syrup, and vanilla with an electric mixer on medium speed until light and fluffy. Add the flour, oats, and salt to the sugar mixture and mix until well blended. Stir in the walnuts. Drop by teaspoonfuls 2 inches apart onto cookie sheets that have been coated with nonstick vegetable cooking spray. Bake for 12 to 15 minutes or until set. Let the cookies cool on cookie sheets for about 2 minutes, then remove to a wire rack to cool completely.

NOTE: You can substitute pancake syrup for real maple syrup. The flavor isn't as strong, but they're still yummy.

Granola Cookies

about 3 dozen cookies

*Here's a cookie for your kids' lunchboxes. They'll make **everybody** happy!*

½ cup (1 stick) butter,
    softened
⅓ cup granulated sugar
⅓ cup firmly packed brown
    sugar
½ teaspoon vanilla extract
1 egg

2 cups Nature Valley® cereal,
    any flavor, slightly crushed
1 cup all-purpose flour
½ teaspoon baking soda
¼ teaspoon baking powder
¼ teaspoon salt

Preheat the oven to 350°F. In a large bowl, combine the butter, sugars, vanilla, and egg. Stir in the remaining ingredients. Drop dough by rounded teaspoonfuls about 2 inches apart onto ungreased cookie sheets. Bake for about 12 minutes or until set but not hard. Cool for 1 minute, then remove from cookie sheets.

Drop by Drop

Chocolate Coconut Crunchers

4½ to 5 dozen cookies

Even if you have only a box of cake mix on hand and no flour, you can still make cookies. Here's a recipe that'll make you a hero (and it's easy, too).

1 package (18.25 ounces)
  German chocolate
  cake mix
1 cup (2 sticks) butter,
  softened
2 eggs
1 cup flaked coconut

1 cup chopped walnuts
1 cup crushed corn flakes
1 cup rolled oats
1 cup (1 6-ounce package)
  semisweet chocolate chips
1 to 2 tablespoons sugar

Preheat the oven to 350°F. In a large bowl, combine the cake mix, butter, and eggs; mix well. Add the coconut, walnuts, corn flakes, rolled oats, and chocolate chips; mix well. Drop the dough by rounded teaspoonfuls 2 inches apart onto ungreased cookie sheets. Flatten the cookies with a glass repeatedly dipped in the sugar. Bake for 8 to 12 minutes or until set. Cool for 1 minute, then remove the cookies from the cookie sheets.

NOTE: Try replacing the German chocolate cake mix with other flavored mixes. Try anything from white to carrot cake mix.

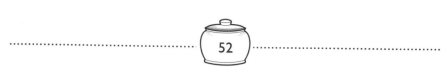

Blondie Chippers

about 5 dozen

Remember the cookies Mom had waiting for us after school? How 'bout baking a memory today?

2¾ cups all-purpose flour
½ teaspoon baking soda
1 teaspoon salt
½ cup granulated sugar
1 cup firmly packed brown
    sugar

½ cup (1 stick) butter,
    softened
2 eggs
1 cup evaporated milk
1 cup (1 6-ounce package)
    semisweet chocolate chips

Preheat the oven to 350°F. In a large bowl, combine the flour, baking soda, salt, and sugars. Blend in the remaining ingredients. Drop by teaspoonfuls onto greased cookie sheets. Bake for 10 minutes.

Drop by Drop

Pumpkin Oatmeal Cookies

about 5 dozen cookies

The taste of autumn in a cookie. But, of course, you can make them and enjoy that taste year-round.

¾ cup (1½ sticks) butter
1½ cups sugar
2 eggs
1 cup canned solid-pack
 pumpkin
1 teaspoon vanilla extract
1½ cups all-purpose flour
2 teaspoons baking powder

½ teaspoon baking soda
½ teaspoon salt
1 teaspoon ground cinnamon
½ teaspoon ground nutmeg
1½ teaspoons ground cloves
1½ cups quick-cooking oats
½ cup flaked coconut
½ cup chopped walnuts

Preheat the oven to 375°F. In a large bowl, cream together the butter and sugar, then add the eggs, pumpkin, and vanilla, blending well. In a separate bowl, combine the flour, baking powder, baking soda, salt, cinnamon, nutmeg, and cloves; add to the pumpkin mixture and mix well. Mix in the oats, coconut, and walnuts. Drop by teaspoonfuls onto greased cookie sheets. Bake for 10 to 12 minutes.

Ultimate Chocolate Chunks

3 to 4 dozen cookies

Chocolate chip cookies are always the rage, and lately they're being "souped up" with chocolate chunks. That sure is good news for us chocolate fanatics!

2 cups all-purpose flour
1 teaspoon baking soda
½ teaspoon salt
½ cup (1 stick) butter, softened
½ cup vegetable shortening
½ cup granulated sugar
¾ cup firmly packed brown sugar

1 teaspoon vanilla extract
1 egg
2 cups (1 12-ounce package) semisweet chocolate chunks
½ cup chopped nuts (optional)

Preheat the oven to 375°F. In a medium-sized bowl, combine the flour, baking soda, and salt; set aside. In a large bowl, combine the butter, shortening, sugars, and vanilla; beat until creamy. Beat in the egg, then gradually add the flour mixture, mixing well. Stir in the chocolate chunks and nuts with a wooden spoon; mix well. Drop by rounded teaspoonfuls 2 inches apart onto ungreased cookie sheets. Bake for 8 to 10 minutes. Cool on cookie sheets for 2 minutes, then remove cookies to a wire rack to cool completely.

Drop by Drop

Piña Colada Cookies

about 7 dozen cookies

These are a super crowd-pleaser, but don't be afraid to cut the recipe in half for a smaller family gathering.

4 cups all-purpose flour
½ teaspoon salt
1½ teaspoons baking soda
½ teaspoon baking powder
1 cup vegetable shortening
1 cup granulated sugar
1 cup firmly packed brown
    sugar

2 eggs
1 can (20 ounces) crushed
    pineapple, undrained
1½ teaspoons vanilla extract
½ cup flaked coconut

Preheat the oven to 350°F. In a medium-sized bowl, combine the flour, salt, baking soda, and baking powder. In a large bowl, cream together the shortening and sugars until light and fluffy. Add the eggs, pineapple, and vanilla; beat thoroughly. Gradually add the flour mixture and blend. Drop the mixture by teaspoonfuls onto cookie sheets that have been coated with nonstick vegetable cooking spray. Sprinkle each cookie with a pinch of coconut. Bake for 12 to 15 minutes or until golden. Cool slightly and remove from the pan with a spatula.

NOTE: I like to substitute rum extract for the vanilla extract, for that real tropical island flavor.

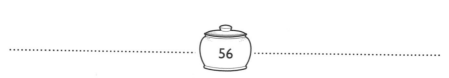

Orange Chocolate Drops

about 2½ dozen cookies

How 'bout the taste of a cheesecake in a cookie? You've got it with these!

½ cup (1 stick) butter,
    softened
12 ounces cream cheese,
    softened
½ cup confectioners' sugar
1 egg
1 tablespoon grated orange
    peel

1 teaspoon vanilla extract
1 cup all-purpose flour
½ teaspoon salt
1 cup (1 6-ounce package)
    semisweet chocolate chips

Preheat the oven to 350°F. In a large bowl, cream the butter and cream cheese until fluffy. Gradually add the confectioners' sugar and egg and blend until smooth. Blend in the orange peel and vanilla, then add the flour and salt. Fold in the chocolate chips. Drop by teaspoonfuls onto greased cookie sheets. Bake for 15 to 20 minutes until set.

NOTE: These cookies are very light in color, so don't expect them to brown too much (except on the bottoms and sides).

It's best not to substitute margarine for butter in this recipe.

Drop by Drop

Chocolate Oatmeal Freckles

about 5 dozen cookies

If you like the rich tastes of chocolate and butterscotch, these are for you . . .

1 cup (2 sticks) butter, softened
1¼ cups firmly packed brown sugar
½ cup granulated sugar
2 eggs
2 tablespoons milk
2 teaspoons vanilla extract

1¾ cups all-purpose flour
1 teaspoon baking soda
¼ teaspoon salt
2½ cups rolled oats
1 cup (1 6-ounce package) semisweet chocolate chips
1 cup butterscotch chips
1 cup chopped walnuts

Preheat the oven to 375°F. In a large bowl, beat the butter and sugars until creamy. Add the eggs, milk, and vanilla; beat well. Add the flour, baking soda, and salt; mix well. Stir in the oats, chocolate and butterscotch chips, and the walnuts; mix well. Drop by rounded tablespoonfuls onto ungreased cookie sheets. Bake for 9 to 10 minutes. Cool for 1 minute, then remove to a wire rack to cool completely.

NOTE: Baking these for 9 to 10 minutes will give you chewy cookies. If you prefer them crispier, bake them for an additional 2 to 3 minutes . . . it's up to you.

Drop by Drop

Glazed Mincemeat Drops

about 3 dozen cookies

A good old-fashioned cookie, rich with flavor.

2 cups all-purpose flour
1 teaspoon ground cinnamon
¼ teaspoon ground nutmeg
½ teaspoon baking soda
½ teaspoon salt
⅔ cup butter, softened

⅔ cup firmly packed brown
   sugar
2 eggs
1 cup prepared mincemeat
1 cup chopped pecans

Orange Glaze

2¾ cups confectioners' sugar
3 tablespoons orange juice

2 tablespoons finely grated
   orange peel

Preheat the oven to 375°F. In a large bowl, combine the flour, cinnamon, nutmeg, baking soda, and salt. In another large bowl, cream the butter and brown sugar. Beat in the eggs and mincemeat. Add the flour mixture to the mincemeat mixture, and stir in the pecans. Drop by heaping teaspoonfuls 2 inches apart on cookie sheets that have been coated with nonstick vegetable cooking spray. Bake for 8 to 10 minutes or until the tops are dry and set. Meanwhile, combine the glaze ingredients in a large bowl and mix until smooth. Remove the cookies to a wire rack to cool. Spread the glaze over the hot cookies. Let stand until the cookies cool completely and the glaze is set.

NOTE: Be sure to glaze the cookies while they're still warm to really blend the flavors.

Original Toll House Chocolate Chip Cookies

about 5 dozen cookies

Everyone's heard of Toll House Chocolate Chip Cookies, right? Of course! We all know the rich taste, but do you know the story behind them? It all started back in the 1930s. In 1930, Ruth Wakefield, proprietress of the Toll House Inn, was experimenting with a favorite colonial cookie. She cut a bar of Nestlé semisweet chocolate into tiny bits and added them to the cookie dough, expecting them to melt. Instead of melting into the dough, the bits of chocolate held their shape and the Toll House cookie was born . . . and are we all glad! This is the actual recipe—I'm not one to mess with tradition, especially since it has long been one of America's favorite treats!

2¼ cups all-purpose flour
1 teaspoon baking soda
1 teaspoon salt
1 cup (2 sticks) butter, softened
¾ cup granulated sugar
¾ cup firmly packed brown sugar

1 teaspoon vanilla extract
2 eggs
2 cups (1 12-ounce package) semisweet chocolate chips
1 cup chopped walnuts or other nuts

Preheat the oven to 375°F. In a small bowl, combine the flour, baking soda, and salt; set aside. In a large bowl, beat the butter, sugars, and

 Cookie Jar Favorite

Drop by Drop

the vanilla until creamy. Beat in the eggs. Gradually blend in the flour mixture. Stir in the chocolate chips and nuts. Drop by rounded measuring tablespoonfuls onto ungreased cookie sheets. Bake for 9 to 11 minutes until the edges are golden brown.

NOTE: If you want a chewier cookie, use ½ cup granulated sugar plus 1 cup firmly packed light brown sugar instead of the sugars listed. If you like a puffier cookie, use ½ cup butter plus ½ cup vegetable shortening instead of only butter.

No-Bake, No-Hassles

Who says all cookies have to be baked? This can be our "secret" chapter, because you're going to hear so many oohs and ahhs and everyone will be saying, "Where did you learn to bake such fancy cookies?" Only you will know that you didn't even have to turn on the oven . . . so just smile and say, "It's a secret from an old friend!!"

Tips

*   Make certain that the recipe has time to set completely before cutting or serving.

*   For the freshest flavor, slice the rolled or bar cookies with a sharp knife right before serving.

*   If wrapped tightly, these cookies will last for several weeks in the refrigerator, which makes them perfect for that drop-in company. So, don't be afraid to make a double batch!

No-Bake, No-Hassles

Cookie Jar Favorites

Church Windows⊕

about 2 dozen cookies

These are guaranteed to be a holiday favorite that you'll want to make all year long.

½ cup (1 stick) butter, softened
1 package (12 ounces) semisweet chocolate chips
1 teaspoon vanilla extract

1 cup chopped walnuts
1 bag (10.5 ounces) multicolored miniature marshmallows
1 cup flaked coconut, divided

In a large saucepan, melt the butter and chocolate chips over low heat until completely melted. Remove the saucepan from the heat and stir in the vanilla and walnuts. Cool the mixture for about 15 minutes, until cool but not to the point of hardening. Fold in the marshmallows and stir until well coated. Spoon half of the mixture lengthwise down the center of a 12-inch piece of waxed paper. Shape into a 12" x 2" log and place at one edge of the waxed paper. Sprinkle ½ cup coconut over the remainder of the waxed paper. Roll the log over the coconut, evenly coating the outside of the entire log. Wrap the log firmly in the waxed paper, folding the ends snugly. Repeat with the other half of the marshmallow mixture and ½ cup of coconut. Refrigerate until firm, at least 2 hours or overnight. Unwrap each log and cut into ¼-inch slices.

NOTE: These are perfect to brighten up your cookie trays. The colors are just like stained glass church windows.

 Cookie Jar Favorite

No-Bake, No-Hassles

Peanut Butter Balls

about 6 dozen cookies

Make any day a celebration with these easy, crunchy treats.

- 1 cup (2 sticks) butter, softened
- 2 cups peanut butter
- 1 box (16 ounces) confectioners' sugar
- 3 cups crisp rice cereal
- 1 package (12 ounces) semisweet chocolate chips
- ½ stick paraffin

In a large bowl, mix the softened butter, peanut butter, confectioners' sugar, and cereal. Chill the mixture for about 1 hour, then roll into 1-inch balls. In a double boiler or a medium-sized saucepan, melt the chocolate chips and paraffin over low heat. Dip the balls into the melted chocolate, using a fork or slotted spoon. Cool on waxed paper.

NOTE: Paraffin can usually be found in the baking or canning section of the supermarket.

It's best not to substitute margarine for butter in this recipe.

No-Bake Granola Bars

16 bars

What a great way to enjoy the crunchy goodness of granola. Indulge yourself!

½ cup semisweet chocolate
   chips
⅔ cup raspberry jam
2 cups granola

½ cup chopped walnuts
½ teaspoon vanilla extract
1 cup crispy rice cereal

In a medium-sized saucepan, heat the chocolate chips and raspberry jam over low heat, stirring constantly until melted and smooth. Remove from heat and stir in the remaining ingredients. Spread the mixture evenly over the bottom of a greased 8-inch square baking pan. Refrigerate for about 1 hour or until firm. Cut into 2-inch squares.

NOTE: Don't have raspberry jam? No problem—use strawberry, mixed berry, or whatever else you have on hand.

No-Bake, No-Hassles

Apricot Macadamia Snowballs

2 dozen

Wow, how can something so easy be so flavorful? Try it and you'll see . . .

6 ounces dried apricots
¼ cup apricot jam
1 tablespoon sugar

1 cup macadamia nuts
½ cup flaked coconut

In a food processor, blend the apricots, jam, sugar, and nuts, pulsing the motor until the mixture forms a mass. Form rounded teaspoonfuls of the mixture into 1-inch balls; roll each ball in the coconut until well coated. Refrigerate for 1 hour.

NOTE: If you prefer a nuttier flavor, you can toast the coconut before using it. Just spread it out on a cookie sheet and place the sheet in a 300°F. oven for about 5 minutes, or until lightly browned.

No-Bake, No-Hassles

Date-Nut Crunchies

about 2½ dozen cookies

When's the last time you had a date with a nut? It's a great combo!

1 cup chopped dates	2 cups crisp rice cereal
½ cup (1 stick) butter	1 cup chopped walnuts
1 egg	1½ cups flaked coconut
¾ cup sugar	

In a medium-sized saucepan, combine the dates, butter, egg, and sugar over low heat. Bring to a boil, stirring constantly, and boil for 5 minutes. Remove from the heat and stir in the cereal and nuts. Cool for 5 to 7 minutes. Form the dough into 1-inch balls and roll in the coconut.

No-Bake, No-Hassles

Butterscotch Yule Log Slices

about 20 cookies

"Yule" love the ease, they'll love the taste.

1 cup (1 6-ounce package)
    butterscotch chips
⅓ cup sweetened condensed
    milk

½ teaspoon vanilla extract
½ cup chopped pecans
1 egg white, lightly beaten
1 can (4 ounces) pecan halves

In the top of a double boiler or in a stainless steel bowl set over a saucepan of simmering water, melt the butterscotch chips until smooth. Stir in the sweetened condensed milk and vanilla. Stir in the chopped pecans, mixing well, and chill until firm enough to handle. Form into a 10-inch long roll on waxed paper. Roll tightly in the waxed paper to shape evenly. Unwrap and mark the surface lengthwise with the tines of a fork, and brush with the egg white. Press the pecan halves into the roll to completely cover the surface, and rewrap in waxed paper. Chill for 2 hours or overnight. Cut into ½-inch slices with a sharp knife.

NOTE: These will hold for several weeks in the refrigerator if kept tightly wrapped and not sliced until used.

Cookie Jar Favorite

No-Bake, No-Hassles

Cookie Clusters

4 to 5 dozen cookies

Sweet, crunchy, and no baking. Now, that's my kind of cookie.

12 ounces white chocolate melting wafers, chips, or squares
2 tablespoons peanut butter

1¼ cups crisp rice cereal
1 cup Spanish peanuts
1 cup miniature marshmallows

Melt the chocolate with the peanut butter in a microwave (or in a saucepan over low heat, stirring frequently); do not allow the mixture to boil. Let cool slightly, then stir in the cereal and peanuts. Fold in the marshmallows, then drop the mixture by teaspoonfuls onto waxed paper. Allow to cool at room temperature for at least 20 minutes before serving. These will keep up to 2 weeks in the refrigerator.

NOTE: You might want to add some fun and color by sprinkling on a little flaked coconut, colored sprinkles, or chopped Heath® candy bars before allowing to cool.

Molasses Coconut Balls

about 3½ dozen cookies

This is another great summer cookie, because no oven means a cool kitchen!

½ cup (1 stick) butter
2 tablespoons orange juice
1 cup all-purpose flour
½ cup maple syrup
¼ cup molasses
¼ teaspoon salt
½ teaspoon ground cinnamon

¼ teaspoon ground ginger
¼ teaspoon ground nutmeg
2 teaspoons vanilla extract
1¼ cups flaked coconut,
    divided
2 cups crisp rice cereal
1½ cups raisins

Melt the butter in a medium-sized saucepan. Stir in the orange juice, flour, maple syrup, molasses, salt, cinnamon, ginger, and nutmeg. Cook over medium heat, stirring constantly, until the dough leaves the sides of the pan and forms a ball. Remove from the heat. Stir in the vanilla and 1 cup of coconut. Cool, then add the cereal and raisins, mixing well. Shape into 1-inch balls; cover and refrigerate for 1 hour. Roll each ball in the remaining coconut. Store in the refrigerator.

No-Bake, No-Hassles

Fun Treats for Kids

What kid doesn't like to help Mom or Dad, big brother, or sister in the kitchen? Sure, not only do they like to eat these incredible edibles, they love to help create them, too. But before getting started, please review these simple rules to ensure big smiles and, yup, of course lots of **OOH it's so GOOD!!**™

Tips

- Always have adult supervision when handling knives, appliances, and the stove and oven.

- Wash hands before starting.

- Read the ingredient list and help check that everything is available.

- Have Mom or Dad preheat the oven, if needed.

- Be a good helper by working alongside Mom or Dad, and help measure, mix, and bake the cookies as the recipe says.

- Only lick extra batter off spoons if it's okay with Mom or Dad.

- Make sure Mom or Dad uses pot holders when putting pans in and taking pans out of the oven. Never do this by yourself.

- Clean up the counters and dirty dishes.

- When directions say so, put cookies on a cooling rack.

- Decorate cookies, whenever appropriate. Yippee! Be creative and have fun.

- Eat a warm (not hot!) cookie to make sure they're yummy, then let the rest cool completely and place them in a cookie jar or wrap properly and store for later.

Fun Treats for Kids

Cookie Jar Favorites

More S'Mores

8 sandwich cookies

*Remember making these over a campfire while listening to ghost stories? Here's a way to make them indoors and make some fun memories for **your** kids.*

8 graham cracker squares, split in half along the perforation

2 milk chocolate candy bars (1.45 ounces each)

8 large marshmallows

Preheat the oven to 350°F. Arrange 8 graham cracker halves on a cookie sheet that has been coated with nonstick vegetable cooking spray. Break each candy bar into 4 even pieces. Place 1 piece of the chocolate on each graham cracker. Cut each marshmallow into quarters and place 4 quarters on top of each piece of chocolate. Top with the remaining graham cracker halves to make sandwiches. Bake for 4 minutes or until the marshmallows and chocolate are slightly melted. Serve immediately, while still warm.

NOTE: You can fancy these up by using chocolate bars that have nuts, rice crisps, or other good stuff!

Fun Treats for Kids

Soft Peanut Butter Cookies

about 2 dozen cookies

*Cookies made without flour? Sure! They'll be **your** favorites 'cause they're a snap, and they'll be the kids' favorites 'cause they're made with peanut butter!*

1 cup sugar	1 egg
1 cup creamy peanut butter	1 teaspoon vanilla extract

Preheat the oven to 325°F. In a medium-sized bowl, mix all the ingredients thoroughly. Drop the mixture by teaspoonfuls onto a nonstick baking sheet and press a crisscross pattern into each drop with a fork. Bake for about 10 minutes or until light golden. Cool before removing from the baking sheet.

NOTE: For a little variety, try pressing colored coated candies into the cookies immediately after removing them from the oven. Kids of all ages love them!

Thumbprint Cookies

about 2 dozen cookies

They're almost as much fun to make as they are to eat.

1 cup sugar
½ cup (1 stick) butter
1 egg
2 teaspoons vanilla extract, divided

2 cups all-purpose flour
2 tablespoons milk
½ cup finely chopped walnuts
¼ to ⅓ cup fruit preserves for filling

Preheat the oven to 350°F. In a large bowl, combine the sugar, butter, egg, and 1 teaspoon of the vanilla. Add the flour, milk, and remaining 1 teaspoon of vanilla; mix well. Shape into balls, then roll the balls in the chopped walnuts. Place on cookie sheets that have been coated with nonstick vegetable cooking spray. Press thumb into the center of each cookie ball to make an indentation, then fill each "imprint" with your favorite preserves. Bake for 15 to 20 minutes or until light golden.

NOTE: The amount of preserves you'll use will depend upon the size of your thumbprints! And be sure to use preserves 'cause jams and jellies tend to liquefy while baking.

   It's best not to substitute margarine for butter in this recipe.

 Cookie Jar Favorite

Haystacks

about 2 dozen cookies

Kids just love dropping these onto the cookie sheets. And boy, are they proud when "their" cookies come out of the oven!

⅔ cup sweetened condensed
   milk
1 cup flaked coconut

1 cup chopped dates
1 cup chopped walnuts
1 teaspoon vanilla extract

Preheat the oven to 350°F. In a medium-sized bowl, combine all the ingredients and mix well. Drop by teaspoonfuls onto a well-greased cookie sheet. Bake for 12 minutes. Remove from cookie sheets immediately and cool on wire racks.

Peanut Butter Crispy Treats

about 32 treats

Kids and peanut butter—it's always been a winning combination.

1 cup light or dark corn syrup   6 cups crisp rice cereal
1 cup sugar
1 cup creamy or crunchy-
    style peanut butter

In a large saucepan, over low heat, mix the corn syrup, sugar, and peanut butter, stirring constantly. Bring to a boil and remove from the heat. Add the cereal and toss to coat well. Immediately press the mixture into a well-greased 9" x 13" baking pan. Cool, then cut into squares.

Cookie in a Cookie

about 3 dozen

Have you ever had a cookie baked in a cookie? You will now!

1 package (18.5 ounces)
white cake mix
⅓ cup vegetable oil

2 eggs
1 cup crushed chocolate
sandwich cookies

Preheat the oven to 350°F. In a large bowl, beat the cake mix, oil, and eggs until well mixed. Stir in the crushed chocolate sandwich cookies. Drop by teaspoonfuls 2 inches apart onto a cookie sheet that has been coated with nonstick vegetable cooking spray. Bake for 7 to 10 minutes or until golden. Cool on wire racks.

NOTE: Be adventurous and try different flavor cake mixes and cookies.

81

Dutch Treats

about 4 dozen bars

*These were the first cookies my daughter ever made. Her favorite part was patting the dough into the cookie sheet. (And they're so easy and good that all these years later she **still** loves making them for us.)*

1 cup (2 sticks) butter	½ teaspoon ground cinnamon
1 cup sugar	1 tablespoon water
1 egg, separated	¼ cup finely chopped walnuts
2 cups all-purpose flour	¼ cup colored nonpareils

Preheat the oven to 350°F. Lightly grease a 10" x 15" rimmed cookie sheet. In a large bowl, combine the butter, sugar, and egg yolk. In another large bowl, combine the flour and cinnamon; stir it into the butter mixture. Using your hands, pat the dough into the pan. In a small bowl, beat the water and egg white until frothy; brush it over the dough, then sprinkle the top with nuts and nonpareils. Bake for 20 to 25 minutes or until light golden. Cut immediately into fingerlike bars.

NOTE: Make sure to use the nonpareils found in the baking section, not the candy section, of your grocery store.

 Cookie Jar Favorite

Popcorn Balls

about twenty 2½-inch balls

Kids love popcorn, and they love to help in the kitchen, so this must be a perfect combination!

4 quarts popped popcorn
I cup sugar
⅓ cup light or dark corn
    syrup
⅓ cup water
¼ cup (½ stick) butter

½ teaspoon salt
I teaspoon vanilla extract
Vegetable oil, vegetable
    shortening, or additional
    butter for greasing hands

Place the popped popcorn in a large stainless-steel mixing bowl in a 200°F. oven to keep warm while preparing the coating. In a medium-sized saucepan, stir together the sugar, corn syrup, water, butter, and salt. Cook over medium heat, stirring constantly, until the mixture comes to a boil. Continue cooking without stirring until the temperature reaches 270°F. on a candy thermometer or until a small amount of the syrup mixture dropped into very cold water separates into threads which are hard but not brittle. Remove mixture from the heat. Stir in the vanilla, then slowly pour the syrup over the popcorn, stirring with a wooden spoon to coat every kernel. When the popcorn is cool enough to handle, but still warm, grease your hands and shape the popcorn into 2-inch balls. Let the balls cool at room temperature.

NOTE: Kids, make sure your parents help you because the sugar mixture is very hot.

Surprises

about 2 dozen cookies

Not only is the center of each cookie a surprise, but the recipe is surprisingly simple, too!

1 cup (2 sticks) butter	½ teaspoon salt
½ cup sugar	2 dozen candied cherries
2 teaspoons vanilla extract	1 cup flaked coconut
2 cups all-purpose flour	

Preheat the oven to 350°F. In a large bowl, cream together the butter, sugar, and vanilla. Stir in the flour and salt. Form the dough into 1-inch balls, then press a cherry into the center of each. Reshape each into a ball, completely covering the cherries. Roll the balls in the shredded coconut and place them 2 inches apart on cookie sheets that have been coated with nonstick vegetable cooking spray. Bake for 20 minutes. Cool on wire racks.

NOTE: You can substitute dates, almonds, or walnuts for the candied cherries.

Fun Treats for Kids

Peanut Butter Graham Treats

about 3 dozen cookies

This is a real "hands-on" experience for your little cookie makers.

1¼ cups graham cracker
    crumbs
¼ cup firmly packed light
    brown sugar

¾ teaspoon ground cinnamon
½ cup crunchy peanut butter
⅓ cup light corn syrup
¼ cup confectioners' sugar

In a medium-sized bowl, combine the graham cracker crumbs, brown sugar, and cinnamon. Stir in the peanut butter and corn syrup until well blended. Using your hands, roll the dough by teaspoonfuls into balls; place on cookie sheets and refrigerate until firm. Just before serving, roll each ball in the confectioners' sugar, coating well.

Fun Treats for Kids

Nutty Coconut Fingers

32 fingers

These are as fun to make as they are to eat and, of course, you can use your fingers.

8 slices stale white bread   1 ½ cups flaked coconut
1 can (14 ounces) sweetened   1 cup ground walnuts
    condensed milk

Preheat the oven to 325°F. Remove the crusts from the bread and cut each slice into 4 strips. Pour the milk into a shallow bowl. In a shallow pan, combine the coconut and walnuts. Dip each bread stick into the milk, then into the coconut mixture, coating all sides. Place each stick on a cookie sheet that has been coated with nonstick vegetable cooking spray. Bake for 12 to 15 minutes or until delicately browned. Remove at once and transfer to a rack to cool and crisp.

NOTE: It is important that the bread be stale and dry, so if yours isn't, you can dry it in a 200°F. oven for 1 ½ to 2 hours.

Fun Treats for Kids

Elfin Crispy Cake

24 servings

Here's the perfect dessert for your little elves to help you make for the holidays.

8 cups *unsweetened* cereal (your elf's favorite)

½ cup (1 stick) butter, melted

½ cup firmly packed light brown sugar

1 package (10 ounces) marshmallows

1 teaspoon vanilla extract

1 cup unsalted nuts

1 cup (1 6 ounce package) semisweet chocolate chips

Coat a large bowl with nonstick vegetable cooking spray. Fill the bowl with the cereal; set aside. In a large skillet, combine the butter and brown sugar over medium heat, stirring constantly until the sugar is dissolved. Add the marshmallows, stirring until the mixture is smooth. Remove from the heat and stir in the vanilla. Immediately pour the mixture over the cereal and stir until well coated. Stir in the nuts and chocolate chips. Press the mixture into a 9" x 13" baking pan that has been coated with nonstick vegetable cooking spray. Set aside for 2 hours before cutting and serving.

NOTE: If you'd like, you can use chocolate-coated candies, gum-drops, or any other type of candy instead of the chocolate chips.

Fun Treats for Kids

Roll-outs

Here's a chapter dedicated to those cookies you may have shied away from making before, except maybe around the holidays. Well, you'll be surprised what you'll be able to do with just a little practice.

The idea is easy: Using a rolling pin to roll out your chilled dough, simply cut out cookies with a cookie cutter or a knife and bake. Of course, each recipe will explain the specific details and, with the help of a few tips, you're guaranteed to be a roll-out cookie pro in no time.

Tips

- Do not attempt to bake roll-outs in a hot and humid kitchen. If the dough is too warm, it will not cooperate.

- Before rolling, lightly dust the countertop or rolling board and rolling pin with flour to prevent the dough from sticking.

- Roll out small amounts of dough at a time, storing the balance in the refrigerator until ready to use.

- Dough should be firm but not hard when it's rolled out.

- When rolling the dough, press down lightly with just enough pressure to stretch it.

- If the dough becomes too wet and sticky, sprinkle it with flour.

- If the dough is soft and sticky, try rolling it between two pieces of waxed paper.

- Do not overwork the dough with your hands because your body heat will warm the dough.

- If you don't have any cookie cutters, try using the top of a clean, smooth-edged, empty small food can. Frozen juice containers work really well!

- If the dough sticks to cookie cutters or knives, dip them in flour and try again.

- Use a wide spatula to transfer cut-out dough to cookie sheets.

Roll-outs

Cookie Jar Favorites

Cream-Filled Cookie Bites

about 40 sandwich cookies

Good thing these are so easy to make, 'cause they seem to disappear as fast as you make them.

Cream Filling

¼ cup (½ stick) butter, softened

¾ cup confectioners' sugar

¾ teaspoon vanilla extract

Cookies

1 cup (2 sticks) butter, softened

⅓ cup heavy cream

2 cups all-purpose flour

⅓ cup granulated sugar

In a medium-sized bowl, cream together the filling ingredients until smooth and fluffy. Cover and chill until ready to use. Meanwhile, in another medium-sized bowl, combine the 1 cup butter, cream, and flour, mixing thoroughly. Cover and chill for about 30 minutes. Preheat the oven to 375°F. Divide the dough into quarters, then remove one quarter at a time from the refrigerator and do the following: Roll it to a ⅛-inch thickness on a floured board. Cut the flattened dough into 1½-inch circles. Use a spatula to transfer the rounds to a piece of waxed paper that has been heavily covered with the granulated sugar. Turn each round so that both sides are coated with sugar. Place on an ungreased cookie sheet. Poke each round with a fork 3 or 4 times. Bake for 7 to 9 minutes, or until set but not brown. When cooled, make a sandwich by placing a dollop of the filling between 2 cookies. Repeat until all cookies and cream have been combined.

Cookie Jar Favorite

Pistachio Pick-ups

about 5 dozen pick-ups

Fancy looking and fancy tasting, but easy, easy, easy!

¾ cup (1½ sticks) butter
½ cup sugar
1 egg

½ teaspoon vanilla extract
2 cups all-purpose flour
⅛ teaspoon salt

Topping

2 tablespoons sugar
½ teaspoon ground cinnamon
¼ cup finely chopped
   pistachios

1 egg white, lightly beaten

In a large bowl, cream the butter, then add the ½ cup sugar, whole egg, and vanilla. Beat until light. Add the flour and salt, blending well. Chill for several hours or until firm enough to roll. Preheat the oven to 350°F. On a floured surface, roll out the dough to a ⅛-inch thickness, then cut into 1" × 2" strips. Place the strips on ungreased cookie sheets. In a small bowl, combine the 2 tablespoons sugar, cinnamon, and pistachios. Brush the dough strips with the egg white, then sprinkle with the topping mixture. Bake for 8 minutes, until light golden. Cool slightly and remove from cookie sheets.

Quick Cookies

about 80 cookies

There's nothing like homemade butter cookies, especially when they're this quick!

1 pound (4 sticks) butter,
  slightly softened
1 cup sugar

5 cups all-purpose flour
½ teaspoon salt

Preheat the oven to 350°F. In a large bowl, beat the butter and sugar with an electric mixer until well mixed. Stir in the flour and salt. Divide the dough in half. Roll out each half on a lightly floured surface to a ⅜-inch thickness. Using cookie cutters or drinking glasses, cut into desired shapes. Place the shapes on ungreased cookie sheets and prick the top of each with a fork. Bake for 25 to 30 minutes, or until lightly browned. Cool completely.

NOTE: Enjoy these as is, or decorate as desired. Add sprinkles while still warm, but add frosting after cookies have completely cooled.

Fruit Foldovers

4 loaves, 10 to 12 servings per loaf

Rich, homemade taste that really satisfies.

2 cups all-purpose flour
¾ cup granulated sugar
¼ teaspoon salt
2 tablespoons baking powder

2 eggs
¼ cup vegetable oil
¼ cup milk
½ teaspoon vanilla extract

Fruit Filling

1 cup prune butter
¼ cup chopped walnuts
¼ cup grape jelly

1 jar (6 ounces) maraschino
   cherries, chopped

Glaze Topping

½ cup confectioners' sugar
1 teaspoon butter, melted

1½ tablespoons milk

Preheat the oven to 350°F. In a large bowl, combine the flour, granulated sugar, salt, and baking powder. Add the eggs, oil, ¼ cup milk, and vanilla; mix well and set aside. In a medium-sized bowl, combine the fruit filling ingredients; set aside. Knead the prepared dough, adding flour if needed. Divide the dough into fourths. Roll each fourth into a rectangular shape to about a ½-inch thickness. Spread one-fourth of the filling lengthwise along the center of each of the four rectangles. Fold the sides and ends over the filling to form a loaf. Place the folded sides down on greased cookie sheets. Bake for 15 to 20 minutes or until golden. Cool. In a small bowl, combine all the topping ingredients. Mix well, drizzle over the fruit loaves, and cut into 1½-inch slices.

Roll-outs

Zesty Honey Crisps

about 2 dozen crisps

You'll love the big lemon taste with the hint of honey . . . so pucker up.

½ cup (1 stick) butter,
    softened
¼ cup firmly packed dark
    brown sugar
2 tablespoons honey
1 tablespoon grated lemon
    rind

½ teaspoon lemon extract
½ teaspoon vanilla extract
1 cup all-purpose flour
¼ teaspoon salt

Glaze

½ cup confectioners' sugar

1 tablespoon fresh lemon
    juice

Preheat the oven to 325°F. In a medium-sized bowl, beat the butter and brown sugar with an electric mixer until light and fluffy. Beat in the honey, lemon rind, lemon extract, and vanilla. Add the flour and salt; blend well. (If dough is too soft, refrigerate for 30 minutes before rolling out.) With a rolling pin, on a lightly floured surface, roll out the dough to a ¼-inch thickness. Cut out the cookies using a 2-inch round cutter and place 2 inches apart on ungreased cookie sheets. Reroll the dough scraps and repeat. Bake for 20 to 25 minutes or until cookies are golden. Cool for 2 minutes and remove to a wire rack to cool completely. Make the glaze by combining the confectioners' sugar and fresh lemon juice and mixing until smooth. Drizzle glaze over each cookie.

NOTE: *Don't substitute lemon juice for lemon extract in this recipe!*

Real Butter Cookies

4 to 6 dozen cookies

Crisp butter cookies like Mama used to make. Mmm, they melt in your mouth.

1½ cups (3 sticks) butter	2 teaspoons vanilla extract
1 cup sugar	¼ teaspoon salt
1 egg	4½ cups all-purpose flour

In a large bowl, beat the butter, sugar, egg, vanilla, and salt with an electric mixer. Gradually add the flour; beat until well mixed. Refrigerate the dough for 1 hour. Preheat the oven to 375°F. Separate the dough into 4 pieces, then roll out each piece on a lightly floured surface to a ¼-inch thickness. Cut or mold the dough into desired shapes. Place the shapes on ungreased cookie sheets and bake for 8 to 10 minutes, or until light brown.

NOTE: The size of the cookie cutters you use will determine the yield. (That's why there's such a wide range given on the yield!)

It's best not to substitute margarine for butter in this recipe.

Roll-outs

European Wine Biscuits

about 5 dozen biscuits

These are like the fancy ones you buy at those expensive import stores, but these are better 'cause you make them right in your own kitchen.

1 cup (2 sticks) butter,
   softened
1 cup sweet red wine
1½ cups granulated sugar
1 tablespoon plus 1 teaspoon
   baking powder

1 teaspoon salt
4 cups all-purpose flour
1 teaspoon vanilla extract
1 cup confectioners' sugar

Preheat the oven to 350°F. In a large bowl, combine the butter, wine, and granulated sugar until well blended. Add the baking powder, salt, flour, and vanilla, mixing until well blended. With a rolling pin, roll out the dough onto a floured board to a ¼-inch thickness. Cut out the cookies with a 2-inch cookie cutter. Place on cookie sheets that have been coated with nonstick vegetable cooking spray. Bake for 15 to 18 minutes. Let cookies cool for 5 minutes. Shake a few cookies at a time in a plastic bag with the confectioners' sugar until well coated. Repeat until all the cookies are coated.

NOTE: Any wine will work in this recipe, but I prefer to use a sweet red wine!

Gingerbread People

20 to 22 figures

*A holiday treat for **every** little Hansel and Gretel.*

1½ cups molasses
1 cup firmly packed brown
   sugar
⅔ cup cold water
⅓ cup butter, softened
6 cups all-purpose flour

2 teaspoons baking soda
1 teaspoon salt
1 teaspoon ground allspice
2 teaspoons ground ginger
1 teaspoon ground cloves
1 teaspoon ground cinnamon

In a large bowl, combine the molasses, brown sugar, water, and butter. Add the remaining ingredients and blend well. Cover and refrigerate for 2 hours. Preheat the oven to 350°F. Divide the dough in half. On a lightly floured surface, roll the dough to a ½-inch thickness. Cut with 7-inch figurine cookie cutters. Place on greased cookie sheets and bake for 10 to 12 minutes. Remove to wire racks and cool, then decorate with icing, if desired.

NOTE: If you'd like to use raisins for the eyes and red cinnamon candies for buttons, press them lightly into the dough before baking. This dough will hold well in the refrigerator for a few days, so you can make it in advance at your convenience.

 Cookie Jar Favorite

Roll-outs

Cheesy Wafers

about 7 dozen wafers

Cheese in cookies?? It sounds crazy, but wait till you try these. They're perfect for an easy hors d'oeuvre or dessert cookie.

¾ cup (1½ sticks) butter, softened
2 cups all-purpose flour
½ teaspoon ground nutmeg
¼ teaspoon cayenne pepper

4 cups (1 pound) coarsely grated sharp Cheddar cheese
¼ cup sugar

Preheat the oven to 400°F. In a large bowl, with your hands, rub together the butter, flour, nutmeg, and cayenne pepper until smooth and creamy. Add the cheese and knead on a piece of waxed paper for 3 to 4 minutes until smooth and thoroughly blended. Divide the dough in half. Using a rolling pin, roll the dough to a ⅛-inch thickness between 2 sheets of waxed paper. Cut with a 2-inch round cookie cutter and sprinkle the cookies generously with sugar. Reroll the dough scraps and repeat. Bake on ungreased cookie sheets for 4 to 6 minutes or until golden. Remove at once to a wire rack to cool.

NOTE: Try using Monterey Jack, Swiss, or any other semi-firm cheese.

It's best not to substitute margarine for butter in this recipe.

Rugelach

5 to 6 dozen cookies

Wait till they smell these—they'll come running! (What makes these more fun to make than Grandma's recipe? There's ice cream in the dough!)

1 pound (4 sticks) butter, softened	½ cup finely chopped nuts (any kind)
4 cups all-purpose flour	¼ cup ground cinnamon
1 pint vanilla ice cream, softened	About ⅔ cup raspberry jelly
1½ cups sugar	About 1¼ cups raisins

In a large bowl, cut the butter into the flour. Add the softened ice cream and work it into the mixture with your hands. (Add more flour if necessary to make the dough easier to handle.) Cover and refrigerate the dough overnight (it will become hard). The following day, preheat the oven to 350°F. In a medium-sized bowl, combine the sugar, nuts, and cinnamon. Sprinkle about one-fifth of the sugar-nut mixture onto a clean pastry cloth, smooth dish towel, or smooth surface. Lightly flour a rolling pin; break off about one-fifth of the dough. Place the dough on the sugar-nut mixture and roll it out (to about ⅛- to ¼-inch thickness) to form a circle. Spread about 2 tablespoons jelly and about ¼ cup raisins over the rolled dough. Cut dough into small pie slice–shaped pieces (about 12 to 14 pieces) and roll up each piece from the outside to the center. Place the rolls seam-side down on a cookie sheet that has been coated with nonstick vegetable cooking spray. Repeat the process, placing more sugar-nut

 Cookie Jar Favorite

Roll-outs

mixture on your smooth surface each time before rolling out the dough into circles, covering each dough circle with the jelly and raisins. Bake for about 30 minutes or until the bottoms turn golden brown.

NOTE: You can leave out the raisins if you prefer, but the flavor and texture are best with them.

Shapely Shapes

Shaped cookies, molded cookies—creative cookies! These are stiffer doughs that can be hand rolled or shaped to create many different shapes. Your whole gang will be impressed that each cookie is hand-made, and you'll be impressed that it's all so easy!

Tips

- Lightly dust your hands with flour or confectioners' sugar to prevent the dough from sticking.

- If the dough seems dry, moisten your hands slightly with a few drops of water.

- Make each batch of cookies uniform shapes and sizes, so they bake evenly.

- Do not overhandle the dough. Work quickly so the warmth of your hands does not warm up the dough and make it difficult to work with.

- If the dough gets too sticky, put it into the refrigerator until it becomes more workable.

- If cooled cookies stick to a cookie sheet, return the pan to a warm oven for about 1 minute, then immediately remove the cookies with a spatula. The time needed will vary, depending on the oven temperature and specific cookies.

Shapely Shapes

 Cookie Jar Favorites

Shapely Shapes

Chocolate Blossoms

about 2 dozen cookies

If there were an Olympics for cookies, these sure would earn a gold medal!

⅓ cup baking cocoa
¼ cup (½ stick) butter, melted
1 cup all-purpose flour, divided
1 cup granulated sugar

2 eggs
1 teaspoon almond extract
1 teaspoon baking soda
¼ teaspoon salt
¼ cup chopped almonds
¼ cup confectioners' sugar

In a large bowl, stir the cocoa into the melted butter. Cool slightly, then stir in ½ cup flour, the granulated sugar, eggs, almond extract, baking soda, and salt. Beat until well blended. Stir in the remaining ½ cup flour and the almonds until blended. Cover and refrigerate the dough until firm, at least 3 hours or overnight. Preheat the oven to 300°F. Shape the dough into 1-inch balls and roll each ball in confectioners' sugar. Place the balls 3 inches apart on a cookie sheet that has been coated with nonstick vegetable cooking spray. Bake for 10 to 12 minutes or until set and the tops have cracked. Immediately remove from cookie sheets and cool on a wire rack.

NOTE: I recommend placing the confectioners' sugar in a shallow pie plate and rolling each cookie to completely cover it.

Cookie Jar Favorite

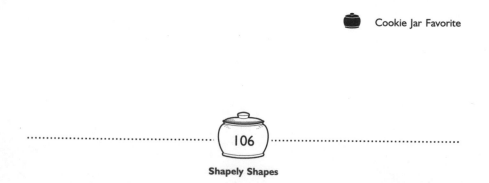

Shapely Shapes

French Lace Cookies

about 4 dozen cookies

Delicious, and so delicate looking on a dessert plate. You'll surely get lots of requests for **this** *recipe.*

I cup all-purpose flour
I cup finely chopped walnuts
½ cup light corn syrup

½ cup (I stick) butter
⅔ cup firmly packed brown
  sugar

Preheat the oven to 375°F. In a medium-sized bowl, combine the flour and walnuts; set aside. In a large saucepan, over medium heat, combine the corn syrup, butter, and brown sugar and bring to a boil, stirring constantly. Remove from the heat and gradually stir in the flour and nuts. Drop batter by teaspoonfuls onto lightly greased cookie sheets, making sure to place only 6 cookies spaced 3 inches apart on each cookie sheet. Bake for 5 to 6 minutes. Remove from the oven and let stand for 3 to 4 minutes before removing from the cookie sheets.

NOTE: The traditional way to finish these is to roll each cookie around the handle of a wooden spoon after they've been out of the oven for 2 to 3 minutes. (They're too soft to handle just out of the oven, but if you wait <u>too</u> long, they stiffen and won't bend around the handle.) Place them on a serving plate and watch them disappear!

It's best not to substitute margarine for butter in this recipe.

Tropical Treats

2½ to 3 dozen cookies

A Hawaiian travel brochure . . . a plate of Tropical Treats . . . and a Fuzzy Navel Froth (page 247). The perfect afternoon getaway.

I cup all-purpose flour
½ teaspoon baking powder
½ cup vegetable oil
3 tablespoons (from a 4-serving size box) orange-flavored gelatin
I package (4-serving size) instant vanilla pudding
¼ cup milk
½ teaspoon orange extract
2 eggs, separated
¾ cup chopped macadamia nuts
I package (7 ounces) flaked coconut, divided
I teaspoon water

Preheat the oven to 350°F. In a large bowl, combine all the ingredients except the egg whites, nuts, coconut, and water. Blend well. Stir in the nuts and ⅔ cup coconut. Using your hands, shape into 1-inch balls. Slightly beat the egg whites with the water. Roll the balls in the egg whites, then in the remaining coconut. Place on ungreased cookie sheets, pressing down to flatten. Bake for 15 to 18 minutes or until light brown. Remove to a wire rack to cool.

NOTE: Maybe change the flavor of the cookies by substituting your favorite flavor of gelatin. Wow, the possibilities are almost endless.

Buried Treasures

about 3½ dozen cookies

Your little pirates will love hunting for these chocolate treasures. (And make sure they leave the treasure map so you can share in the bounty!)

¾ cup (1½ sticks) butter
½ cup granulated sugar, plus extra for rolling
¼ cup firmly packed brown sugar
1 egg
2 teaspoons vanilla extract

1¾ cups all-purpose flour
½ teaspoon baking powder
½ teaspoon salt
3½ dozen foil-wrapped milk chocolate candies, unwrapped

Preheat the oven to 350°F. In a large bowl, with an electric mixer, cream together the butter, ½ cup granulated sugar, and the brown sugar until light and fluffy. Add the egg and vanilla and beat well. Mix in the flour, baking powder, and salt, blending well. Form the dough into 1-inch balls; press a candy piece into each ball, covering the candy completely with dough. Roll the balls in granulated sugar and place on ungreased cookie sheets. Bake for 12 minutes or until light golden.

Chinese Almond Rounds

3 to 4 dozen cookies

Enjoy this light treat with your favorite after-dinner tea.

¾ cup sugar plus extra for
   dipping
1 teaspoon baking powder
¾ cup (1½ sticks) butter,
   softened

1 egg
2 tablespoons water
1 teaspoon almond extract
2½ cups all-purpose flour
⅓ cup whole shelled almonds

Preheat the oven to 350°F. In a large bowl, combine the ¾ cup sugar, baking powder, butter, egg, water, and almond extract on medium speed with an electric mixer; blend well. Gradually add the flour, blending on low speed until well mixed. Shape the dough into 1-inch balls and place about 2 inches apart on greased cookie sheets. Flatten the balls slightly with a glass repeatedly dipped in the extra sugar; press a whole almond firmly into the center of each cookie. Bake for 8 to 12 minutes until firm to the touch but not brown. **Do not overbake**. Immediately remove from the cookie sheets and cool on wire racks.

NOTE: If you think these are good with almond extract, you won't believe how flavor-packed they can be with raspberry extract. You've got to try that, too.

Nice-Spice Cookies

2½ to 3 dozen cookies

These are perfect for sharing with that special someone in front of the fireplace on a cold winter night.

¾ cup vegetable shortening
1 cup sugar
1 egg
¼ cup light molasses
2 cups all-purpose flour

2 teaspoons baking soda
¼ teaspoon salt
1 teaspoon ground cinnamon
½ teaspoon ground cloves
¾ teaspoon ground ginger

Preheat the oven to 375°F. In a large bowl, cream the shortening, sugar, egg, and molasses until light and fluffy. In another large bowl, combine the remaining ingredients. Add the flour mixture to the shortening mixture, mixing well. Form into 1-inch balls and place 2 inches apart on cookie sheets that have been coated with nonstick vegetable cooking spray. Bake for 10 to 12 minutes or until golden. Cool slightly then remove to a wire rack to cool completely.

NOTE: Don't be afraid to cut down on any of the spices if you prefer them less spicy.

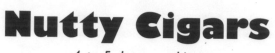

Nutty Cigars

4 to 5 dozen cookies

You can pass out **these** *cigars on* **any** *occasion!*

1 cup (2 sticks) butter at
    room temperature
2 cups all-purpose flour
⅔ cup granulated sugar
¼ cup finely chopped
    almonds

Confectioners' sugar for
    sprinkling
Ground cinnamon for
    sprinkling

Preheat the oven to 375°F. In a large bowl, combine the butter, flour, granulated sugar, and almonds and blend well. Cover and chill the dough in the refrigerator until firm, at least 1 hour or overnight. With your hands, form the dough into small balls, then roll into cigar shapes. Place them on cookie sheets that have been coated with nonstick vegetable cooking spray. Bake for 15 minutes or until golden. Cool, then sprinkle with confectioners' sugar and cinnamon.

NOTE: For more festive cookies, tint the dough with a few drops of red food color for Valentine's Day, green for St. Patrick's Day, and, of course, a batch of each color for Christmas!

Cottage Cheese Cookies

about 7 dozen cookies

My mom used to make these for my aunt, who liked a very soft cookie that wasn't too sweet.

1 cup (2 sticks) butter, melted
1½ cups granulated sugar
⅛ teaspoon salt
2 tablespoons baking powder
5 cups all-purpose flour

4 eggs
1 pound cottage cheese, undrained
1 tablespoon milk
4 teaspoons vanilla extract
½ cup confectioners' sugar

Preheat the oven to 350°F. In a large bowl, combine the melted butter, granulated sugar, salt, baking powder, flour, and eggs until blended. Stir in the cottage cheese, milk, and vanilla. Roll the dough into 1½-inch balls and place on cookie sheets that have been coated with nonstick vegetable cooking spray. Bake for 10 to 12 minutes or until golden. Let stand for 2 minutes, then sprinkle with the confectioners' sugar and cool on a wire rack.

NOTE: These cookies don't freeze well, so you'd better invite a whole gang over to help eat 'em all!

Shapely Shapes

Chocolate-Dipped Walnut Shortbread Wedges

about 32 cookies

These taste like the ones they make in French pastry shops, and now we know how easy they are . . .

1¼ cups (about 6 ounces) shelled walnuts

1¼ cups all-purpose flour plus extra for dusting

¾ cup sugar

1¼ sticks (10 tablespoons) butter

¾ cup (4 ounces) semisweet chocolate chips

1 tablespoon vegetable shortening

Preheat the oven to 350°F. In a food processor, finely grind the walnuts, 1¼ cups flour, and sugar, using the cutting blade. Add the butter and blend until well mixed. Coat two 8-inch round cake pans with nonstick vegetable cooking spray and dust lightly with flour. Press half of the dough into each pan, evenly covering the pan bottoms. With a small knife, score each pan of dough into 16 wedges. Bake in the middle of the oven for 20 minutes or until golden brown. While the shortbread is still warm, cut through the scored lines and allow to cool in the pans on a wire rack. In a small heavy saucepan, melt the chocolate chips and shortening, stirring until smooth. Dip the points of the cooled shortbread wedges into the chocolate mixture, coating them halfway, allowing any excess to drip off. Put the dipped wedges on a wire rack over waxed paper and allow to set.

NOTE: Be careful not to cut through the dough when scoring it before baking.

Shapely Shapes

Molasses Crackle

about 5 dozen cookies

Watch out! You may not have time to get these into the cookie jar, 'cause as soon as they're ready, they'll be gone.

¾ cup (1 ½ sticks) butter
¾ cup sugar plus ½ cup
   for rolling
¼ cup dark molasses
1 egg
2 teaspoons baking soda

2 cups all-purpose flour
½ teaspoon ground cloves
½ teaspoon ground ginger
1 teaspoon ground cinnamon
½ teaspoon salt

In a large saucepan, melt the butter; let cool. Add the remaining ingredients except the ½ cup sugar for rolling; mix well by hand. Refrigerate for 2 hours. Preheat the oven to 375°F. Roll the dough into ½-inch balls, then roll in the granulated sugar and place on a lightly greased cookie sheet. Bake for 10 to 12 minutes. Cool on the cookie sheet for 1 minute, then carefully remove to wire racks. Cookies will harden as they cool.

Shapely Shapes

All-American Cookies

about 3 dozen cookies

Here's a cookie that brings together that great American combination of apples and Cheddar cheese.

I cup sugar, divided
¾ teaspoon ground cinnamon
¼ teaspoon ground nutmeg
I teaspoon vanilla extract
2½ cups all-purpose flour
¼ teaspoon salt

¾ cup (1½ sticks) butter, softened
⅓ cup applesauce
¾ cup shredded sharp Cheddar cheese

Preheat the oven to 350°F. In a small bowl, combine ½ cup sugar, the cinnamon, and nutmeg; set aside. In a large bowl, combine the remaining ingredients, except the cheese, and mix well. Gradually add the cheese and stir until evenly blended. Roll the dough into balls and place 2 inches apart on ungreased nonstick cookie sheets. Flatten the cookies with a fork and sprinkle generously with the sugar mixture. Bake for 12 to 14 minutes or until golden. Remove from the cookie sheets while still warm.

NOTE: Use mild or sharp Cheddar if you prefer. Make them *your* way.

Anise Biscuits

about 3 dozen biscuits

Here's an easy, one-step biscotti that's a super little "dunker" for coffee or tea. In fact, in Italy they serve biscuits like these for breakfast!

2¼ cups all-purpose flour
2 heaping teaspoons baking
    powder
1 cup sugar

2 teaspoons anise seed
⅛ teaspoon salt
2 eggs
½ cup vegetable oil

Preheat the oven to 350°F. In a large bowl, mix the flour, baking powder, sugar, anise seed, and salt. Add the eggs and oil and mix until well blended. Roll the dough into 1-inch balls, then form into cigar shapes. Place on an ungreased cookie sheet and bake for 10 to 15 minutes, until light golden.

Shapely Shapes

Split Seconds

about 30 bars

Wanna make a contest winner from 1954 that's still a winner today? Just ask your family to judge for themselves.

¾ cup (1½ sticks) butter, softened
⅔ cup sugar
1 egg
2 teaspoons vanilla extract

2 cups all-purpose flour
½ teaspoon baking powder
⅓ cup strawberry, raspberry, or apricot jam

Preheat the oven to 350°F. In a large bowl, blend the butter, sugar, egg, and vanilla. With an electric mixer on low speed, add the flour and baking powder; mix well. Place the dough on a lightly floured board and divide it into 4 equal parts. Shape each part into a roll approximately 12 inches long and ¾ inch thick. Place the rolls on an ungreased cookie sheet about 4 inches apart and 2 inches from the edge of the pan. Using a wooden spoon handle, make a lengthwise depression in the center of each roll, about ¼- to ⅓-inch deep, lengthwise. Fill the depressions with jam and bake for 15 to 20 minutes or until golden. While still warm, cut diagonally into ¾-inch slices.

NOTE: You can use your finger or a knife handle to make the depressions in the dough if you don't have a wooden spoon.

Cookie Jar Favorite

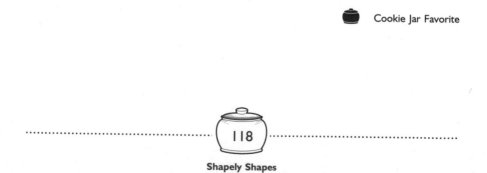

Shapely Shapes

Chocolate Peanut Butter Jewels

about 2½ dozen cookies

Lock these in a safe place or they'll be gone before you know it!

1½ cups all-purpose flour
1½ teaspoons baking powder
¼ teaspoon salt
1 cup (1 6-ounce package) semisweet chocolate chips
2 tablespoons butter, softened

1 cup granulated sugar
1½ teaspoons vanilla extract
2 egg whites
¼ cup water
1 cup (1 6-ounce package) peanut butter chips
½ cup confectioners' sugar

In a medium-sized bowl, combine the flour, baking powder, and salt; set aside. In a small heavy saucepan, melt the chocolate chips over low heat until smooth. In a large bowl, cream the butter, granulated sugar, and vanilla until light and fluffy. Beat in the melted chocolate chips and the egg whites. Gradually beat in the flour mixture, alternately with the water. Stir in the peanut butter chips. Cover and chill for at least 45 minutes or until firm. Preheat the oven to 350°F. Shape the dough into 1½-inch balls. Roll in the confectioners' sugar, coating generously. Place on a cookie sheet that has been coated with nonstick vegetable cooking spray. Bake for 10 to 15 minutes or until the sides are set, but the centers are still slightly soft. Cool.

NOTE: The chocolate chips can be melted in the microwave (in a microwave-safe bowl) for about 2 to 3 minutes. The time will vary depending upon the strength of your microwave, so keep an eye on them!

Shapely Shapes

French Butter Creams

about 4 dozen cookies

Ooh la la! These are melt-in-your-mouth wonderful!

1½ cups confectioners' sugar
1 teaspoon baking soda
1 teaspoon cream of tartar
1 teaspoon salt
1 cup (2 sticks) butter,
   softened

1 egg
1 teaspoon vanilla extract
2¼ cups all-purpose flour

In a large bowl, with an electric mixer on low speed, mix all the ingredients except the flour. Gradually add the flour and mix until well blended. Chill the dough for 30 minutes. Preheat the oven to 350°F. Shape the dough into ¾-inch balls and place 2 inches apart on greased cookie sheets. Flatten the balls with a fork. Bake for 5 to 8 minutes until set but not brown. Let cool on the cookie sheets for 1 minute, then transfer to wire racks to cool. Store loosely covered.

NOTE: If you'd like, tint the dough by blending in a few drops of food color after adding the flour. Or, just before baking, sprinkle the tops lightly with colored granulated ("crystal") sugars (found in your supermarket baking section).

Toasted Almond Horseshoes

about 3 dozen cookies

Playing horseshoes might be challenging, but keeping these horseshoe-shaped cookies from disappearing is even more of a challenge.

1 cup (2 sticks) butter,
    softened
⅔ cup confectioners' sugar
1 teaspoon vanilla extract
1 teaspoon almond extract
½ teaspoon salt

1¾ cups all-purpose flour
1 cup coarsely chopped
    toasted almonds
½ cup semisweet chocolate
    chips

Preheat the oven to 325°F. In a large bowl, cream the butter and confectioners' sugar until light and fluffy. Beat in the vanilla and almond extracts, salt, and flour until thoroughly blended. Stir in the almonds. Make a 1-inch ball of the dough and roll out into a 2-inch rope using the palms of your hands. Place on ungreased cookie sheets, curving each piece of the dough into a horseshoe shape. Bake for 15 to 18 minutes or until golden. Immediately remove to a wire rack to cool. When cool, dip the points of the horseshoes into chocolate chips that have been melted in the microwave or in a saucepan over low heat. Then place the finished cookies on waxed paper until the chocolate hardens.

NOTE: To chop the almonds, I like to use a small food processor.

Shapely Shapes

Twisted Chocolate Pretzel Cookies

about 32 pretzel cookies

Pretzels and ice cold milk . . . it's an interesting combination that really works. Wait till you try **these**!

1⅔ cups all-purpose flour
¼ cup baking cocoa
¾ cup butter, softened
½ cup granulated sugar
¼ cup firmly packed brown
    sugar

1 teaspoon vanilla extract
1 egg, separated
3 tablespoons milk
6 to 7 sugar cubes, coarsely
    crushed

Preheat the oven to 350°F. In a small bowl, combine the flour and cocoa and set aside. In a large bowl, beat together the butter, granulated and brown sugars, vanilla, egg yolk, and milk until blended. Gradually blend in the flour mixture until smooth. Cover the bowl with plastic wrap and refrigerate for 1 hour. Then divide the dough into 4 even pieces and divide each quarter into 8 even pieces. Roll each piece on a lightly floured board with the palm of your hand until approximately 8 inches long. Twist each into a pretzel shape. Place 1 inch apart on a cookie sheet that has been coated with nonstick vegetable cooking spray. Lightly beat the egg white and brush it over the "pretzels"; sprinkle with the crushed sugar cubes. Bake for 12 to 14 minutes, until the cookies are firm when lightly touched. Let cool slightly, then remove to a wire rack.

NOTE: Prefer pretzel sticks to pretzel twists? Go ahead and shape them however you'd like—they'll still have the same fun flavor.

Cherry Winks

about 4 dozen cookies

Easy as can be and fruit-chunky, too. What are you waiting for?

1 cup sugar
¾ cup (1½ sticks) butter
2 eggs
1 teaspoon vanilla extract
2¼ cups all-purpose flour
1 teaspoon baking powder
½ teaspoon salt

1 cup chopped walnuts
1 cup chopped dates
½ cup chopped maraschino
  cherries
1 cup finely crushed corn
  flakes

Preheat the oven to 375°F. In a large bowl, cream together the sugar and butter. Add the remaining ingredients except the crushed corn flakes, and blend well. Form the dough into 1-inch balls, then roll the balls in the crushed corn flakes. Place on ungreased cookie sheets and bake for 12 to 15 minutes, until light golden. Immediately remove from cookie sheets and cool on wire racks.

Shapely Shapes

Pecan Butter Balls

about 2 dozen balls

A rich buttery taste studded with chopped pecans . . . bet ya' they'll melt in your mouth.

¼ cup plus 2 tablespoons sugar	¾ cup (1½ sticks) butter, softened
1 cup finely chopped pecans	⅛ teaspoon salt
1 teaspoon vanilla extract	1 cup all-purpose flour

Place the ¼ cup sugar in a shallow pan and set aside. In a large bowl, combine the remaining ingredients. With your hands, mix until thoroughly blended; cover and refrigerate the dough for 30 minutes. Preheat the oven to 375°F. Form the dough into 1¼-inch balls, then roll in the reserved sugar, covering completely. Place 1 inch apart on an ungreased cookie sheet. Bake for 15 to 20 minutes or until set but not brown. Let stand for 1 minute. Remove to a wire rack to cool.

NOTE: It's best not to substitute margarine for butter in this recipe.

Ginger Cocoa Crisps

2½ to 3 dozen cookies

The great homemade taste of ginger snaps, with a chocolate twist.

¾ cup (1½ sticks) butter
1 cup sugar plus ¼ cup for
    rolling
1 egg
¼ cup molasses

2 cups all-purpose flour
¼ cup baking cocoa
1½ teaspoons baking soda
2½ teaspoons ground ginger
½ teaspoon salt

Preheat the oven to 350°F. In a large bowl, cream the butter; slowly add the 1 cup sugar, beating with an electric mixer at medium speed until light and fluffy. Add the egg, beating well. Stir in the molasses, then set aside. In another large bowl, combine the flour and cocoa, then stir in the baking soda, ginger, and salt; add to the molasses mixture, mixing well. Shape the dough into 1-inch balls, then roll in the reserved ¼ cup sugar. Place 2 inches apart on lightly greased cookie sheets. Bake for 10 to 12 minutes. Cool completely on wire racks.

Shapely Shapes

Double Chocolate Peanut Butter Thumbprints

about 3½ dozen cookies

Wanna make a batch of cookies that will earn a "thumbs up"? Here it is!

1½ cups all-purpose flour
⅓ cup baking cocoa
1½ teaspoons baking powder
¼ teaspoon salt
2 cups (1 12-ounce package) semisweet chocolate chips, divided

1 cup sugar
1 cup chunky or smooth peanut butter, divided
⅓ cup butter, softened
1½ teaspoons vanilla extract
2 eggs

In a medium-sized bowl, combine the flour, cocoa, baking powder, and salt. In a small saucepan over low heat, melt 1 cup chocolate chips; stir until smooth. In a large bowl, cream the sugar, ⅓ cup peanut butter, butter, and vanilla. Beat in the melted chocolate. Add the eggs one at a time, beating well after each addition. Gradually beat in the flour mixture. Stir in the remaining chocolate chips. Cover and chill just until firm. Preheat the oven to 350°F. Shape the dough into 1½-inch balls, press your thumb into the tops to make ½-inch deep depressions. Place on ungreased baking sheets and fill each depression with about ½ teaspoon peanut butter. Bake for 10 to 15 minutes or until the sides are set but the centers are still slightly soft. Cool for 2 minutes. Remove to wire racks to cool completely.

NOTE: All-natural peanut butter doesn't work in this recipe.

Shapely Shapes

Lemony Oat Cookies

about 4 dozen cookies

I love to dunk these in a glass of hot tea or spiced apple cider . . . Mmm!

2 cups (4 sticks) butter, softened
1 cup granulated sugar
2 cups all-purpose flour
3 cups rolled oats
1 tablespoon grated lemon peel
2 teaspoons lemon extract
½ cup chopped candied cherries
⅓ cup confectioners' sugar

In a large bowl, beat the butter and granulated sugar until creamy. Add the remaining ingredients except the confectioners' sugar; mix well. Cover and chill for 30 minutes. Preheat the oven to 350°F. Shape the dough into 1-inch balls and place on ungreased cookie sheets. Flatten with the bottom of a glass repeatedly dipped in confectioners' sugar. Bake for 12 to 15 minutes or until the edges are golden. Cool for 1 minute on the cookie sheets, then remove to a wire rack to cool completely. Sprinkle with additional confectioners' sugar, if desired.

NOTE: If you'd prefer these without the chopped candied cherries, no problem—just leave them out.

Shapely Shapes

Pecan Coconut Rounds

about 4 dozen cookies

With this combination of coconut, pecans, and honey, you're gonna hear lots of lip-smackin' **OOH it's so GOOD!!**™

3 cups rolled oats	1 teaspoon vanilla extract
1 cup flaked coconut	1 cup (2 sticks) butter
1 cup pecan pieces	⅓ cup honey
¼ teaspoon ground cinnamon	24 maraschino cherries, cut
1 cup all-purpose flour	in half
1⅓ cups firmly packed light brown sugar	

Preheat the oven to 350°F. In a large bowl, combine the oats, coconut, pecans, cinnamon, and flour. In a medium-sized saucepan, combine the remaining ingredients except the cherries, and bring to a boil over medium heat. Pour the honey mixture over the flour mixture and blend until well mixed. Lightly grease 48 muffin pans, then fill each one-third full with batter. Top each with a cherry half and bake for about 12 minutes until the edges brown. Let cool slightly and remove from pans with a butter knife.

NOTE: Sshh, my secret of using the muffin tins makes these cookies perfectly round. (No, they won't rise like regular muffins.)

Shapely Shapes

Icebox Favorites

These could be called icebox or refrigerator cookies, and they're often confused with shaped or molded cookies, since some of those are also refrigerated to firm up the cookie dough and to help it hold its shape. But icebox cookies are great for unexpected company because the dough can be made in advance and kept ready and waiting in the refrigerator (for up to three days) to be dropped or thinly sliced and baked. The dough can be held in the freezer for several months if wrapped tightly in waxed paper and aluminum foil.

Tips

- Be certain that firm add-ins such as nuts and chocolate chunks are chopped small enough to allow the dough to be cut or dropped easily.

- If dough becomes too soft to handle, return it to the refrigerator for several minutes.

- If you don't have time to wait for the dough to firm up in the refrigerator, simply drop the dough with a teaspoon, instead of slicing, and bake according to directions. The baking time might alter slightly, so check them carefully.

- Most dough can be cut while still partially frozen, then baked within several minutes of thawing. Again, check the cookies carefully since baking time may vary.

- Several recipes with firm dough throughout this book will also work well as icebox cookies. For example, the Incredible Chocolate Chunks cookie dough (page 33) will hold for several days in the refrigerator by rolling it into a 2-inch round log and wrapping it tightly in waxed paper. Then simply cut it into $1/4$-inch slices and bake according to directions.

Icebox Favorites

Cookie Jar Favorites

Hint of Mints

about 5 dozen cookies

These are mighty minty and mighty tasty . . . and they make a mighty big hit every time I make them.

⅔ cup butter, softened
½ cup sugar plus ¼ cup for rolling
1 egg
1¾ cups all-purpose flour
¼ cup light corn syrup
2 teaspoons baking soda

¼ teaspoon salt
1 cup (1 6-ounce package) semisweet chocolate chips
1 cup (6 ounces) chocolate-covered thin mints, *or* ¼ teaspoon mint extract
½ teaspoon vanilla extract

In a large bowl, beat together the butter, ½ cup sugar, and egg. Add the flour, corn syrup, baking soda, and salt. In a small saucepan, over low heat, melt the chocolate chips and thin mints (or simply add the mint extract). Add to the dough mixture with the vanilla, blending well. Chill overnight. Remove the dough from the refrigerator and allow to soften slightly. Preheat the oven to 350°F. Roll the dough into 1-inch balls. Roll the balls in the remaining ¼ cup sugar and place on ungreased cookie sheets. Bake for 10 to 12 minutes, or until the cookie tops crack. When done, the cookies will still be soft to the touch. Allow to cool slightly, then remove to a wire rack to cool.

Cookie Jar Favorite

Vanilla Sugar Cookies

3½ to 4 dozen cookies

This is a versatile cookie 'cause it's perfect as is, or you can use the same dough with other flavorings and come up with really fun variations. I'll show you . . . I'm giving you two for starters—you take it from there!

¾ cup (1½ sticks) butter, softened
1 cup sugar
1 egg

1 teaspoon vanilla extract
⅛ teaspoon salt
2 cups all purpose flour

Preheat the oven to 350°F. In a large bowl, beat together the butter and sugar with an electric beater. Add the egg, vanilla, and salt; beat until smooth. Stir in the flour and knead lightly until a soft dough forms. Divide the dough in half, then wrap each half in waxed paper to form a cylinder about 1½ inches in diameter. Refrigerate the dough until firm, about 2 hours. Cut the dough into ¼-inch slices and arrange on greased cookie sheets. Bake for 12 to 15 minutes.

Orange Poppy Seed Cookies

Mix in 2 tablespoons poppy seed and ½ teaspoon orange extract before adding the flour. Flatten the sides of the wrapped dough to form a rectangular shape before chilling.

Cinnamon Pecan Cookies

Mix in 1 cup chopped pecans before adding the flour. Sprinkle the ¼-inch slices generously with a combination of ½ teaspoon ground cinnamon and ¼ cup sugar before baking.

Icebox Favorites

Spiced Candied Fruit Cookies

about 4½ dozen cookies

No need to wait for the holidays to get the big taste of fruitcake!

1 cup (2 sticks) butter, softened
1 cup sugar
1 egg
½ cup heavy cream
3¾ cups all-purpose flour

1 teaspoon baking powder
1 teaspoon ground cinnamon
½ teaspoon ground ginger
½ teaspoon ground nutmeg
2 cups (12 ounces) chopped mixed candied fruit

In a large bowl, cream the butter and sugar until light and fluffy. Beat in the egg and cream. Mix in the flour, baking powder, cinnamon, ginger, and nutmeg; beat until well combined. Stir in the candied fruit. Divide the dough in half, shaping each half into a 2-inch-diameter log. Wrap in waxed paper and refrigerate overnight or freeze for about 1½ hours. Preheat the oven to 350°F. Cut the rolls into ¼-inch slices and place 1 inch apart on cookie sheets that have been coated with nonstick vegetable cooking spray. Bake for 10 to 12 minutes or until the bottoms are lightly browned. Remove to a wire rack to cool.

NOTE: Make sure you cut this dough with a sharp knife!

Peanut Butter Sandwich Cookies

about 18 sandwiches

Here's something for your family's lunchboxes that you know won't be traded!

1½ cups all-purpose flour
½ cup sugar
½ teaspoon baking soda
½ teaspoon salt

½ cup vegetable shortening
1½ cups creamy or crunchy peanut butter, divided
½ cup light corn syrup

Preheat the oven to 350°F. In a large bowl, combine the flour, sugar, baking soda, and salt. Cut in the shortening and ½ cup peanut butter (the mixture will resemble coarse meal); add the corn syrup, blending well. Form the dough into rolls approximately 2 inches in diameter. Cover a cookie sheet with waxed paper; place the rolled dough on the waxed paper, and chill for at least 1 hour. Remove the dough from the cookie sheet and discard the waxed paper. Coat the cookie sheet with nonstick vegetable cooking spray. Cut the chilled dough into ¼-inch slices and place the slices on the cookie sheet. Place ½ teaspoon of peanut butter on each slice, then top with another slice of cookie dough, pressing down gently on the edges. Bake for 12 to 15 minutes. Cool before removing from the cookie sheets.

NOTE: If you like crunchier cookies, then certainly use chunky peanut butter instead of creamy.

Icebox Favorites

European Chocolate Cookies

about 2½ dozen cookies

Let your taste buds travel to Europe while you and your family travel back and forth to the cookie jar.

1½ cups semisweet chocolate chips, divided

1 square (1 ounce) unsweetened baking chocolate

1 tablespoon unsalted butter

⅓ cup firmly packed dark brown sugar

1 egg

1 tablespoon water

1 teaspoon vanilla extract

2 tablespoons all-purpose flour

⅛ teaspoon baking powder

1 cup coarsely chopped walnuts

In the top of a double boiler, or in a stainless steel bowl set over a saucepan of simmering water, melt ½ cup chocolate chips, the unsweetened chocolate, and the butter over simmering water until smooth and well blended. Transfer the chocolate mixture to a medium-sized bowl and let cool slightly. Blend the brown sugar, egg, water, and vanilla into the slightly cooled chocolate mixture. Stir in the flour and baking powder until well mixed. Stir in the remaining 1 cup chocolate chips and the nuts. (The batter will be very sticky.) Cover and refrigerate for at least 1½ hours, or overnight. Preheat the oven to 350°F. Line 2 cookie sheets with foil. Drop by teaspoonfuls onto the prepared cookie sheets. Bake for 13 to 15 minutes, until the cookies are firm to the touch, reversing the position of the trays once during baking. Remove the cookie sheets to wire racks and cool completely before removing the cookies from the foil.

NOTE: Store in an airtight container to maintain the scrumptious flavor!

 Cookie Jar Favorites

Icebox Favorites

Health Rounds

about 5 dozen cookies

We call these healthy 'cause they're studded with sunflower kernels and raisins . . . a nice change of pace.

½ cup (1 stick) butter, softened	½ teaspoon baking soda
1 cup sugar	¼ teaspoon salt
1 egg	2 cups all-purpose flour
1 tablespoon maple syrup	½ cup sunflower kernels
	½ cup raisins

In a large bowl, combine all the ingredients except the sunflower kernels and raisins; mix well. Add the sunflower kernels and raisins and stir just until evenly mixed. Divide the dough in half. Place each half on waxed paper and shape into 1½-inch diameter rolls. Wrap tightly and chill for 1 hour. Preheat the oven to 375°F. Cut into ⅛-inch slices with a serrated knife. Place on ungreased cookie sheets. Bake for 10 minutes or until golden.

NOTE: Make sure to use sunflower kernels and not sunflower seeds.

Chocolate Confetti Cookies

5 to 6 dozen cookies

Bring back the days of sharing a double-dipped chocolate ice cream cone covered with rainbow sprinkles . . . yes, in a cookie!

1 cup (2 sticks) butter, softened
1½ cups sugar
2 teaspoons vanilla extract
2 eggs
3¾ cups all-purpose flour

1½ teaspoons baking powder
1 teaspoon salt
¾ cup semisweet chocolate chips, melted
1 cup rainbow sprinkles

In a large bowl, cream the butter, sugar, and vanilla until light and fluffy. Add the eggs, beating well. On the lowest speed of an electric mixer, add the flour, baking powder, and salt; blend well. Stir in the melted chocolate chips and the sprinkles; mix well. Divide the dough in half and roll each half into a 2-inch-diameter log. Wrap each log in waxed paper and refrigerate for 1 to 2 hours or freeze for 1 hour, until firm. Preheat the oven to 350°F. Slice cookies ¼ inch thick and place on cookie sheets that have been coated with nonstick vegetable cooking spray. Bake for 8 to 10 minutes or until firm.

NOTE: For a more chocolatey look, use chocolate sprinkles instead of rainbow.

Cookies by the Calendar

We all have special dates on our calendars—why, we live by the calendar! We've got loads of important activities, holidays, and birthdays, and now we can add some fun to those important celebrations by baking "Cookies by the Calendar."

This chapter begins with a New Year's cookie that will start your year off on a sweet note. There are also sweet treats for Super Bowl Sunday, Valentine's Day, and even a "bang" of a cookie for the Fourth of July! Of course, I've got a back-to-school favorite and Halloween and Christmas selections, too. And I'm sure you'll find a cookie **some-where** in this book to name as your own special birthday cookie . . . what will it be?

My gift to you is a choice of yummy new ways to enjoy all your special days. So, the next time you flip through your calendar, don't forget to add a reminder to make your favorite cookies for yet another **OOH it's so GOOD!!**™ day.

Cookies by the Calendar

 Cookie Jar Favorites

Scottish New Year's Crisps

about 40 cookies

*I can't think of a better way to welcome in the New Year than with these Scottish crisps, perfect with champagne **or** a glass of ice cold milk. And no, you don't have to be Scottish to enjoy these.*

½ cup (1 stick) plus 2
    tablespoons butter,
    softened
½ cup plus 2 tablespoons
    sugar

1 egg
1 teaspoon vanilla extract
1½ cups all-purpose flour
¼ teaspoon baking powder
¼ teaspoon salt

Preheat the oven to 300°F. In a large bowl, cream together the butter and sugar, add the egg, and beat until fluffy. Blend in the remaining ingredients. Use a spatula to spread the batter evenly into a 9½" × 13½" rimmed cookie sheet that has been coated with nonstick vegetable cooking spray; smooth the top. (Batter will be firm.) Draw the tines of a fork over the dough to make straight shallow lines going both horizontally and vertically, creating a crisscross pattern. Bake for 30 minutes or to a pale golden color. Remove from the oven and immediately cut into strips. Let cool in pan on a wire rack; when cool, remove carefully. Store in an airtight container.

NOTE: If you don't have a 9½" × 13½" rimmed cookie sheet, you could use a 9" × 13" glass baking dish.

Cookie Pizza

16 servings

*It's a pizza, it's a cookie; it's the perfect dessert for Super Bowl Sunday—
or, if you ask my family, any day.*

½ cup firmly packed brown
  sugar
¼ cup granulated sugar
½ cup (1 stick) butter,
  softened
1 teaspoon vanilla extract
1 egg
1¼ cups all-purpose flour
½ teaspoon baking soda

1 cup (1 6-ounce package)
  semisweet chocolate chips
1 can (16 ounces) white
  frosting
¼ cup chopped walnuts
¼ cup flaked coconut,
  toasted
¼ cup colored coated
  chocolate candies

Preheat the oven to 350°F. In a large bowl, beat the sugars, butter, vanilla, and egg until creamy. Stir in the flour and baking soda until well mixed. (The dough will be stiff.) Stir in the chocolate chips. Spread the dough on an ungreased 12-inch pizza pan or cookie sheet. Bake for 12 to 15 minutes or until golden. When completely cooled, spread frosting over the cookie base, leaving a ¼-inch edge to form the crust. Sprinkle with the walnuts, coconut, and candies. Cut into wedges to serve.

NOTE: Top this dessert pizza with your favorite toppings. There are no rules! Maybe decorate the pizza with jelly beans that match your favorite team colors.

See page 68 for how to toast flaked coconut.

Cookies by the Calendar

Peppermint Kisses

about 2½ dozen cookies

Valentine's Day wouldn't be complete without a kiss . . . a peppermint kiss, that is.

2 egg whites
¼ teaspoon cream of tartar
½ cup sugar

¼ teaspoon peppermint
    extract
3 drops red food color

Preheat the oven to 200°F. In a large bowl, beat the egg whites and cream of tartar with an electric mixer at medium speed until soft peaks form. Add the sugar, 1 tablespoon at a time, beating on high speed. Add the peppermint extract and food color with the last tablespoon of sugar and beat until the sugar is dissolved and stiff peaks form. Drop the mixture by teaspoonfuls to create a "kiss" shape onto cookie sheets that have been lined with foil. Bake for 50 to 60 minutes or until firm. Remove from the cookie sheets and store loosely covered at room temperature.

NOTE: Make sure you do not refrigerate these kisses or they will soften.

Cookies by the Calendar

Hamantaschen

about 2 dozen cookies

These are traditional little pastries made for the festive Jewish holiday of Purim, the Feast of Esther.

½ cup (1 stick) butter
⅔ cup sugar
2 eggs
2¾ cups all-purpose flour

2 teaspoons baking powder
¼ teaspoon salt
½ cup prune, apricot, or
    poppy seed filling

Preheat the oven to 350°F. In a medium-sized bowl, cream the butter and sugar until light and fluffy; add the eggs and beat well. Add the flour, baking powder, and salt and mix well. Shape the dough into 1-inch balls, flattening each with the palms of your hands into round ¼-inch-thick disks. Place 1 teaspoon of the filling into the center of each disk and pinch the edges up in 3 places to form a triangle. Place on cookie sheets that have been coated with nonstick vegetable cooking spray. Bake for 12 minutes or until golden brown. Cool on wire racks.

Cookies by the Calendar

Leprechaun Bits

about 5 dozen cookies

These used to be at the end of the rainbow, but since they disappear so quickly, only the pot of gold is left!

1 cup (2 sticks) butter, softened
2 cups all-purpose flour
⅔ cup granulated sugar
¼ cup finely chopped almonds

1 teaspoon mint extract
3 to 4 drops green food color
Confectioners' sugar for sprinkling

Preheat the oven to 375°F. In a large bowl, combine all the ingredients except the confectioners' sugar, and blend well, mixing by hand until a soft dough forms. Cover and chill the dough until firm. Form the dough into small balls, then place on ungreased cookie sheets and flatten the balls with the palm of your hand. Bake for 15 minutes or until light golden. Cool, then sprinkle with confectioners' sugar.

NOTE: If you want your cookies to be a deeper shade of green, add a few more drops of food color. And if you'd like them really minty, go ahead and add more mint extract, too.

Easter Egg Nests

about 18 small nests

An Easter basket wouldn't be complete without these special treats.

¼ cup sugar
1 egg
1 teaspoon vanilla extract
3 to 4 drops yellow food
   color

¼ cup all-purpose flour
2 cups flaked coconut
36 jelly beans

Preheat the oven to 350°F. In a medium-sized bowl, beat the sugar, egg, vanilla, and food color until well blended. Beat in the flour until smooth, then fold in the coconut. Drop by heaping teaspoonfuls 2 inches apart onto cookie sheets that have been coated with nonstick vegetable cooking spray. With a floured thumb, press an indentation into the center of each cookie mixture to create a nest. Bake for 10 to 12 minutes or until edges are golden. Remove from the oven and gently push 2 jelly beans into each nest. Let the nests cool slightly on the cookie sheets, then remove to wire racks to cool completely. Store in airtight containers.

NOTE: I recommend doubling this recipe because everybody always wants to show off these treats.

"Hoppy" Easter Egg Cookies

5 to 6 dozen cookies

Plan to make these with the whole family, 'cause the icing part is like decorating Easter eggs, but much easier.

1 cup sugar
1 cup (2 sticks) butter, softened
3 tablespoons milk
1 teaspoon vanilla extract
1 egg
3 cups all-purpose flour

1½ teaspoons baking powder
½ teaspoon salt
2 egg yolks
Few drops each of yellow, red, blue, and green food color

In a large bowl, combine the sugar, butter, milk, vanilla, and the egg until well mixed. Stir in the flour, baking powder, and salt; mix well. Cover with plastic wrap. Refrigerate for 1 hour. Preheat the oven to 375°F. On a lightly floured surface, roll out one-fourth of the dough at a time to ⅛-inch thickness. Keep the remaining dough refrigerated. Cut out egg shapes with an oval cookie cutter and place on cookie sheets that have been coated with nonstick vegetable cooking spray. Bake for 6 to 9 minutes or until the edges are light brown. Turn off

 Cookie Jar Favorite

Cookies by the Calendar

the oven. Immediately loosen the cookies, but leave on the cookie sheets. Decorate by beating the egg yolks and dividing them into 4 small cups. Put a few drops of each food color into the separate cups, one color per cup. Using a **new** small model brush, paint each cookie to resemble Easter eggs. Return cookies to the oven for 5 minutes to set the egg paintings.

NOTE: If you don't have an oval cookie cutter, use an empty 6-ounce frozen juice container with the top and bottom removed. Pinch the sides in slightly to make an oval shape and, presto . . . you now have an oval cookie cutter.

Lemonade Cookies

about 4 dozen cookies

Memorial Day marks the beginning of summer, and what better way to start it off than with lemonade? Now you'll taste summer in every bite.

1 cup (2 sticks) butter, softened
1 cup plus 2 tablespoons sugar
2 eggs
3 cups all-purpose flour

1 teaspoon baking soda
1 can (6 ounces) frozen lemonade concentrate, thawed, divided
1 tablespoon grated lemon peel

Preheat the oven to 400°F. In a large bowl, cream together the butter and 1 cup sugar. Add the eggs, beating well. In another large bowl, combine the flour and baking soda and add alternately with ½ cup of lemonade concentrate into the egg mixture. Stir in the lemon peel. Drop by teaspoonfuls 2 inches apart onto ungreased cookie sheets. Bake for 8 to 9 minutes or until edges are light brown. Remove from the oven and brush the hot cookies lightly with the remaining lemonade concentrate. Sprinkle the cookies with the remaining 2 tablespoons sugar.

NOTE: Make sure to thaw the lemonade concentrate in the refrigerator overnight.

Cookies by the Calendar

Fourth of July Cookies

about 3 dozen cookies

Stars and stripes may be forever, but these colorful cookies won't last long at all . . . 'cause of their dynamite taste.

1 package (18.5 ounces)
  white cake mix
2 eggs
⅓ cup vegetable oil
¼ cup crushed red-hot
  cinnamon candies

3 to 4 tablespoons (from a
  4-serving size box)
  blueberry gelatin

Preheat the oven to 350°F. In a large bowl, combine the cake mix, eggs, and oil. Stir in the crushed cinnamon candies. Drop the dough by teaspoonfuls onto cookie sheets that have been coated with non-stick vegetable cooking spray. Sprinkle the tops of the cookies with the gelatin. Bake for 8 to 10 minutes or until light golden. Remove from the cookie sheets to a wire rack to cool.

NOTE: To crush the cinnamon candies, place them in a plastic bag on a cutting board and roll firmly with a rolling pin.

 Cookie Jar Favorite

Back-to-School Cookies

about 4 dozen cookies

Wanna have a great lunchbox cookie that's sure to make the grade?

1 package (18.25 ounces)
   yellow cake mix with
   pudding
⅓ cup vegetable oil
¼ cup firmly packed brown
   sugar

2 eggs
10 graham cracker squares,
   coarsely crushed
½ cup semisweet chocolate
   chips

Preheat the oven to 350°F. In a large bowl, with an electric mixer, combine the cake mix, oil, brown sugar, and eggs. Stir in the cracker crumbs and the chocolate chips. Drop by teaspoonfuls onto cookie sheets that have been coated with nonstick vegetable cooking spray. Bake for 10 to 12 minutes. Remove cookies to wire racks to cool.

NOTE: These freeze really well, so make an extra batch to keep on hand.

Pumpkin Scotchies

about 4 dozen cookies

A dynamic duo that packs a punch of flavor.

1½ cups canned solid-pack
    pumpkin
1 cup sugar
1 teaspoon vanilla extract
2 cups all-purpose flour

1 teaspoon baking soda
1 teaspoon baking powder
1 teaspoon ground cinnamon
1 cup butterscotch chips
1 cup chopped walnuts

Preheat the oven to 350°F. In a large bowl, combine the pumpkin, sugar, and vanilla; add the remaining ingredients and mix well. Drop by teaspoonfuls onto greased cookie sheets. Bake for 12 to 15 minutes or until golden.

NOTE: Try adding some coconut, raisins, or candied fruit, too!

Halloween Bars

2 to 3 dozen bars

Whip up a yummy Halloween treat for your little ghouls and boys!

½ cup (1 stick) butter
1½ cups graham cracker
   crumbs
1 can (14 ounces) sweetened
   condensed milk

2 cups (1 12-ounce package)
   semisweet chocolate chips
1 cup peanut butter chips
½ cup candy corn

Preheat the oven to 325°F. Place the butter in a 9" × 13" baking dish and melt in the oven. Remove the dish from the oven and distribute the melted butter evenly over the bottom. Sprinkle the graham cracker crumbs evenly over the melted butter; pour the sweetened condensed milk evenly over the crumbs. Top with the chocolate chips and peanut butter chips; press down firmly. Bake for 25 to 30 minutes, until golden. Sprinkle with the candy corn and gently press the candies into the uncut bars. Cool, then cut into bars.

153

Hanukkah Cut-outs

about 2 dozen cookies

Celebrate the holiday season with delicious honey-flavored cookies the whole family will love.

½ cup sugar
½ cup (1 stick) butter,
   softened
¼ cup honey
1 egg yolk

1½ cups all-purpose flour
1 teaspoon baking powder
Colored granulated ("crystal")
   sugar (optional)

In a large bowl, beat together the sugar and butter on medium speed with an electric mixer until light and fluffy, 1 to 2 minutes. Add the honey and egg yolk and continue beating, scraping the bowl often, until well mixed, another 1 to 2 minutes. Reduce the speed to low and add the flour and baking powder. Continue beating, scraping the bowl often, until just mixed, about 1 minute. Cover and refrigerate until firm, about 1 hour. Preheat the oven to 400°F. On a lightly floured surface, roll the dough to ⅛-inch thickness. Cut with 2½-inch cookie cutters. Place 1 inch apart on ungreased cookie sheets. Sprinkle with colored sugars, if desired. Bake for 7 to 12 minutes or until the edges are lightly browned. Cool for 1 minute, then remove from the cookie sheets.

NOTE: If the cookies seem to spread, the dough is too soft. Refrigerate the dough until it is well chilled and try again. If you'd like to make traditional holiday shapes, try cookie cutters in the shape of the Star of David, menorahs, and dreidels. And if you'd like, decorate these with frosting after they're completely cool.

Cookies by the Calendar

Candy Cane Cookies

about 4 dozen cookies

Looking for a way to use up those broken candy canes from the holiday? Here it is.

1 cup (2 sticks) butter, softened
1 cup confectioners' sugar
1 egg
½ teaspoon peppermint extract
½ teaspoon vanilla extract

2½ cups all-purpose flour
¼ teaspoon salt
1 cup crushed candy canes
3 tablespoons granulated sugar

Preheat the oven to 375°F. In a large bowl, cream the butter and confectioners' sugar until light and fluffy. Add the egg and the peppermint and vanilla extracts and beat until well blended. Gradually add the flour and salt; mix until thoroughly blended. Cover the bowl tightly with plastic wrap and refrigerate for 1 hour. Shape into 1½-inch balls and roll each ball in a mixture of crushed candy canes and granulated sugar until all the dough has been used. Place on cookie sheets that have been coated with nonstick vegetable cooking spray. Bake for 10 to 12 minutes until browned. Immediately remove from cookie sheets and place on wire racks to cool.

NOTE: Make sure to crush the candy canes well.

Reindeer Cookies

about 5 dozen cookies

*You know how we always leave cookies out for Santa? Well, this year how 'bout leaving **these** out for the reindeer (and all your favorite elves, too)?*

½ cup (1 stick) butter,
    softened
¼ cup light molasses
¼ cup dark molasses
½ cup sugar

1 tablespoon white vinegar
2 cups all-purpose flour
1 teaspoon ground cinnamon
½ teaspoon ground ginger
1½ teaspoons baking soda

In a small saucepan, combine the butter, molasses, sugar, and vinegar. Place over moderate heat and boil gently for 3 minutes, stirring constantly. Remove from the heat and cool. In a medium-sized bowl, combine the remaining ingredients; slowly add to the cooled molasses mixture, stirring constantly until smooth. Shape the dough into 2 balls, wrap both in waxed paper, and chill for several hours or overnight. Preheat the oven to 375°F. On a lightly floured surface, roll out the dough to a ⅛-inch thickness. Cut with a 2-inch round cookie cutter. Place 2 inches apart on cookie sheets that have been coated with nonstick vegetable cooking spray. Bake for 7 to 8 minutes or until a rich brown. Immediately remove from the cookie sheets to cool on wire racks.

Spiced Cherry Bells

about 3½ dozen cookies

Here's a spicy addition for your holiday cookie platter.

3½ cups all-purpose flour
½ teaspoon baking soda
½ teaspoon salt
1 teaspoon ground ginger
½ teaspoon instant granulated coffee
1 cup (2 sticks) butter

1½ cups firmly packed brown sugar
½ cup corn syrup
1 egg
1 tablespoon heavy cream or milk

Nut Filling

⅓ cup firmly packed brown sugar
1 tablespoon butter
1 jar (6 ounces) maraschino cherries

3 tablespoons maraschino cherry juice
1½ cups finely chopped walnuts

In a large bowl, combine the flour, baking soda, salt, ginger, and coffee granules. In a medium-sized bowl, cream the butter, 1½ cups brown sugar, corn syrup, egg, and cream. Add the flour mixture to the butter mixture, blending well. Refrigerate for 3 hours or overnight. Preheat the oven to 350°F. In a medium-sized bowl, combine the filling ingredients; set aside. Roll the dough to a ¼-inch thickness and cut with a bell-shaped or round cookie cutter. Place the shapes on ungreased cookie sheets. Place a teaspoon of the nut mixture in the center of each cookie and add half of a maraschino cherry to make the bell clapper. Bake for 12 to 15 minutes.

NOTE: If using a round cookie cutter, after placing the nut mixture in the center, simply fold in the sides a bit to form a bell shape.

157

Holly Crackles

about 36 cookies

A bright and cheery treat that's fun to serve at holiday time.

½ cup (1 stick) butter
30 large marshmallows
   (1 10-ounce bag contains
   38 to 40)
1 to 1½ teaspoons green
   food color

1½ teaspoons vanilla extract
4 cups corn flakes cereal
Red-hot cinnamon candies,
   for decorating

In a medium-sized saucepan, melt the butter and marshmallows over moderate low heat, stirring constantly. When melted, remove from the heat and stir in 1 teaspoon of food color and the vanilla. Add more food color if desired. Stir in the corn flakes. Drop the mixture, 1 tablespoon at a time, onto waxed paper. Decorate with the candies. Let stand for 30 minutes, until cool.

NOTE: You can make these a springtime treat, too—just use pastel food color and jelly beans and call them Birds' Nests!

These Bars Are Stars

One of my favorite memories from my childhood is of Mom pulling a batch of bar cookies out of the oven. My mom loved making these for us because, as the chapter title says, these bars **are** stars!

There are so many varieties of bar cookies, and they're all quick and easy! With a few simple directions, it'll be no time before you're baking up batch after batch of star bars.

Tips

- Always use the pan size that is indicated. The wrong size pan will create bars that are either underbaked or overbaked, and may completely change the texture.

- Line a pan with foil, then bake according to the recipe directions if you plan to remove the whole batch in one piece for easier storage. Be sure the bars are cool and semifirm before removing, to avoid crumbling.

- When pouring batter into the baking pan, be certain to spread it evenly—and don't forget the corners!

- Let bars cool on a wire cooling rack before cutting, unless the recipe states otherwise.

- Use a sharp knife for cutting and, if the bars are sticky, dip the knife blade into hot water.

- After cutting bars, allow them to cool completely before removing from the pan.

- Remove the corner piece first. That makes it easier to remove the rest of the pieces.

- You can freeze cut bar cookies in the pan, but it's better to freeze them uncut.

These Bars Are Stars

 Cookie Jar Favorites

These Bars Are Stars

White Chocolate Cherry Bars

36 bars

White chocolate and cherries . . . what a combination!

1 cup (2 sticks) butter,
   softened
¾ cup granulated sugar
¾ cup firmly packed brown
   sugar
2 eggs
1 teaspoon vanilla extract
2½ cups all-purpose flour

1 teaspoon baking soda
2 cups (1 12-ounce package)
   white chocolate chips,
   divided
½ cup flaked coconut
½ cup chopped maraschino
   cherries

Preheat the oven to 375°F. In a large bowl, cream the butter and sugars until light and fluffy. Beat in the eggs and vanilla. Mix in the flour and baking soda and beat until well blended. Stir in 1 cup chocolate chips, the coconut, and chopped cherries. Spread the dough evenly into a greased 9" × 13" baking pan. Sprinkle the remaining 1 cup chocolate chips over the dough and bake for 30 to 35 minutes until slightly firm. Cool and cut into bars.

These Bars Are Stars

Almond Florentines

about 6 dozen bars

An elegant delight for the real cookie connoisseurs in your life.

1¼ cups (2½ sticks) unsalted butter, melted
1½ cups sugar
3 cups all-purpose flour
¾ cup cornstarch
¼ teaspoon salt

1 jar (12 ounces) apricot or seedless raspberry preserves or jam (about 1 cup), melted
1⅓ cups sliced almonds

Preheat the oven to 325°F. Line a 10" × 15" rimmed cookie sheet with heavy-duty aluminum foil and allow it to overhang the edges; coat the foil with nonstick vegetable cooking spray. In a large bowl, mix the melted butter, sugar, flour, cornstarch, and salt until well blended. Press the dough evenly into the prepared pan. Bake for 30 minutes. Remove from the oven and spread with the melted preserves. Sprinkle the almonds evenly over the top. Bake for 20 to 30 minutes more or until the edges are golden but not brown. Cool on a wire rack for 15 minutes, then gently slide the foil from the cookie sheet onto a flat surface. When the jam is firm enough to allow easy cutting, cut lengthwise into 1-inch-wide strips, then cut into 2-inch-long cookies.

These Bars Are Stars

Ooey Gooey Chewies

30 bars

The name says it all . . . so make sure you have a tall glass of ice cold milk to wash 'em down!

1 bag (14 ounces) caramels
1 can (5 ounces) evaporated milk, divided
1 package (18.5 ounces) chocolate cake mix with pudding
½ cup (1 stick) butter, melted

1 cup (1 6-ounce package) semisweet chocolate chips
1½ cups chopped pecans, divided
1 cup flaked coconut

Preheat the oven to 350°F. In a small saucepan melt the caramels in ⅓ cup evaporated milk over low heat, stirring occasionally until smooth. Set aside. In a large bowl, mix the remaining evaporated milk, cake mix, and butter. Press half of the batter into the bottom of an ungreased 9" × 13" baking pan. Bake for 10 minutes or until set. Sprinkle with the chocolate chips and 1 cup of the pecans and top with the coconut and the caramel mixture, spreading to the edges of the pan. Top evenly with teaspoonfuls of the remaining cake batter. Sprinkle with the remaining nuts. Bake for 20 to 25 minutes. Cool pan on a wire rack and cut into bars.

NOTE: These are best served warm or at least at room temperature.

These Bars Are Stars

Apple Nut Bars

21 bars

A *is for apple and* A+ *is what you'll get for making these.*

1 cup all-purpose flour	¼ cup (½ stick) butter,
1 cup granulated sugar	melted
½ teaspoon salt	⅓ cup raisins
¼ teaspoon baking powder	1 cup chopped walnuts
2 eggs, well beaten	1 cup finely chopped apples

Preheat the oven to 350°F. In a large bowl, mix the flour, sugar, salt, and baking powder. Add the remaining ingredients and mix well. Place the batter into a greased 9" × 13" baking dish. Bake for 40 to 50 minutes or until the edges are golden. Remove from the oven and cut into bars while still warm, but not hot.

NOTE: Before serving, you might want to roll the bars in confectioners' sugar or spread with a cream cheese frosting. Maybe serve them with whipped topping as a "dip" or serve plain as a great snack cookie.

Zebras

36 bars

A rich bar that has certainly earned its stripes.

1 cup (2 sticks) butter, softened
1 cup firmly packed light brown sugar
2 eggs
1 teaspoon vanilla extract
2 cups all-purpose flour
1 teaspoon baking powder
2 cups (1 12-ounce package) semisweet chocolate chips, divided
¾ cup chopped walnuts

Preheat the oven to 350°F. In a large bowl, cream the butter and brown sugar; beat until light and fluffy. Beat in the eggs, vanilla, flour, and baking powder until well mixed. Melt 1 cup of the chocolate chips in the microwave or over low heat on the stove. Place half of the batter into a medium-sized bowl and stir in the melted chocolate. Spread evenly in a greased 9" × 13" baking pan. Drop tablespoons of the remaining batter over the chocolate batter and drag the blade of a butter knife through the batter to create zebra stripes. Sprinkle with the remaining chocolate chips and the walnuts. Bake for 25 to 30 minutes. Cool completely before cutting into bars.

NOTE: These freeze well if wrapped tightly.

These Bars Are Stars

Coffee Bars

32 bars

Coffee lovers will beg for more of these (and so will the tea and milk lovers).

½ cup (1 stick) butter
2 cups firmly packed brown
   sugar
2 eggs
1 teaspoon vanilla extract
1 cup coffee
3 cups all-purpose flour

¼ teaspoon salt
1 teaspoon baking powder
1 teaspoon baking soda
1 teaspoon ground cinnamon
1 cup raisins
½ cup chopped walnuts

Glaze

½ cup confectioners' sugar
1 tablespoon butter, melted

1 tablespoon milk

Preheat the oven to 350°F. In a large bowl, cream the butter and brown sugar. Mix in the eggs and vanilla, then gradually add the coffee, mixing well. In another large bowl, combine the flour, salt, baking powder, baking soda, and cinnamon; gradually add to the butter mixture. Stir in the raisins and nuts. Pour into a greased 8-inch square baking dish. Bake for 15 to 20 minutes. Meanwhile, in a small bowl, combine the glaze ingredients. Remove the baking dish from the oven and drizzle with the glaze. Cool, then cut into bars.

NOTE: Make sure you use a cup of prepared coffee and not coffee grounds or instant granules.

 Cookie Jar Favorite

These Bars Are Stars

Pecan Fudgies

18 squares

Make way for the chocolate lovers!

2½ cups all-purpose flour
2 cups sugar
¾ cup baking cocoa
1 teaspoon baking soda
1 teaspoon salt
⅔ cup vegetable oil

1 teaspoon vanilla extract
1½ cups cold water
2 eggs
1 cup (1 6-ounce package)
    semisweet chocolate chips
1 cup chopped pecans

Preheat the oven to 350°F. In a large bowl, mix all the ingredients, except the chocolate chips and pecans, until well blended. Pour the mixture into a greased and floured 9" × 13" baking pan. Top with the chocolate chips and pecans. Bake for 35 to 45 minutes or until a wooden toothpick inserted in the center comes out clean. Cool, then cut into squares.

These Bars Are Stars

Yummy Rummy Raisin Bars

25 bars

Bet you can't say "Yummy rummy raisin bars in your tummy" three times fast . . . !

3 tablespoons rum
¾ cup raisins
½ cup (1 stick) butter, softened
⅓ cup granulated sugar
¼ teaspoon vanilla extract

1 egg
1 cup all-purpose flour
½ teaspoon baking powder
¼ cup milk

Rum Glaze

2 tablespoons butter or margarine, softened

1 tablespoon rum
½ cup confectioners' sugar

Preheat the oven to 350°F. In a small bowl, toss the 3 tablespoons rum with the raisins and set aside to soak for 1 hour. In a large bowl, cream the ½ cup butter, granulated sugar, vanilla, and egg until light and fluffy. Stir in the flour and baking powder alternately with the milk, until well mixed. Stir in the rum-soaked raisins, rum and all. Spread the batter evenly into a greased 9-inch square baking dish. Bake for 20 to 25 minutes, or until a wooden toothpick inserted in the center comes out clean. While cooling, combine the glaze ingredients in a small bowl and mix until smooth. While still warm, top the bars with the glaze and cut into squares.

NOTE: If you want a really strong rum flavor, soak the raisins for several hours. And you can use either light or gold rum.

These Bars Are Stars

Hermits

40 squares

Serve up a plateful of these with some cold milk to remind you and your friends of days gone by.

1 cup (2 sticks) butter, softened	1 teaspoon baking soda
2 cups firmly packed light brown sugar	1 teaspoon ground nutmeg
	1 ¼ teaspoons ground cinnamon
2 eggs	3 ½ cups all-purpose flour
½ cup cold water	2 cups raisins

Preheat the oven to 400°F. In a large bowl, with an electric mixer, cream together the butter and brown sugar. Blend in the eggs. On low speed, beat in the water, then the baking soda, nutmeg, and cinnamon. Gradually mix in the flour, one-third at a time. Stir in the raisins. Place the batter in a 10" × 15" rimmed cookie sheet that has been coated with nonstick vegetable cooking spray. Bake for 15 to 18 minutes or until firm. Remove pan to a wire rack to cool.

NOTE: Add some variety by adding your own personal favorites, like maybe chopped dates or cherries in place of the raisins.

 Cookie Jar Favorite

Chocolate Rainbow Bars

3 to 3½ dozen bars

These goodies will bring a ray of sunshine to **anyone's** *face.*

2 cups (1 12-ounce package) semisweet chocolate chips

1 package (8 ounces) cream cheese, softened

1 can (5 ounces) evaporated milk

½ cup chopped walnuts

½ cup rainbow sprinkles

1 teaspoon almond extract, divided

3 cups all-purpose flour

1½ cups sugar

1 teaspoon baking powder

½ teaspoon salt

1 cup (2 sticks) butter, softened

2 eggs

½ teaspoon vanilla extract

Preheat the oven to 350°F. In a medium-sized saucepan, combine the chocolate chips, cream cheese, and evaporated milk. Cook over low heat, stirring constantly, until the chips are melted and the mixture is smooth. Remove from the heat. Add the nuts, sprinkles, and ½ teaspoon almond extract; blend well and set aside. In a large bowl, combine the flour, sugar, baking powder, salt, butter, eggs, vanilla, and the remaining almond extract. Beat with an electric mixer on low speed until the mixture resembles coarse crumbs. Press half of the crumb mixture into an ungreased 9" × 13" baking pan. Spread the chocolate mixture over the crumb mixture. Top with the remaining crumb mixture. Bake for 35 to 40 minutes or until golden. Cool, then cut into bars.

NOTE: The top layer should be a crumby texture. If the dough for the top layer gets soft, pinch off small pieces and place them on top of the chocolate that way.

These Bars Are Stars

New York Cheesecake Squares

16 squares

These could be stars on Broadway . . . and on your kitchen table, too.

1 cup all-purpose flour
⅓ cup butter, softened
⅓ cup firmly packed brown
   sugar
½ cup chopped walnuts
1 package (8 ounces) cream
   cheese, softened

⅓ cup confectioners' sugar
2 tablespoons milk
2 tablespoons lemon juice
½ teaspoon vanilla extract
½ teaspoon grated lemon
   peel
1 egg

Preheat the oven to 350°F. In a large bowl, combine the flour, butter, and brown sugar; beat for about 3 minutes. Stir in the walnuts. Measure out 1 cup of the flour mixture and set aside. Press the remaining flour mixture into an ungreased 8-inch square baking pan to form a crust. Bake for 12 minutes or until light brown. In the same bowl, combine the remaining ingredients and blend well. Pour the cream cheese mixture over the baked crust and sprinkle with the reserved 1 cup of flour mixture. Bake for 25 to 30 minutes or until firm in the center. Let cool on a baking rack then cut into 2-inch squares.

NOTE: Why not top each square with a dollop of your favorite pie filling before serving?

These Bars Are Stars

Date-Nut Bars

18 bars

Oh, boy! These are a traditional favorite 'cause they're so great for munching.

½ cup vegetable shortening
1 cup all-purpose flour
1 teaspoon baking powder
1 teaspoon salt
1¼ cups granulated sugar

4 eggs
1 teaspoon vanilla extract
1½ cups chopped dates
1½ cups chopped walnuts
Confectioners' sugar for
    sprinkling

Preheat the oven to 350°F. In a large bowl, combine all the ingredients except the dates, nuts, and confectioners' sugar; mix well. Mix in the dates and walnuts. Pour the batter into a greased and floured 9" × 13" baking dish. Bake for about 35 minutes. Cool, then cut into 3" × 6" bars. Sprinkle with confectioners' sugar.

Chocolate Crumble Bars

18 bars

Brighten the day for them and for you when you bring a plate of these to the table.

½ cup (1 stick) butter, softened
¾ cup sugar
2 eggs
1 teaspoon vanilla extract
¾ cup all-purpose flour
½ cup chopped pecans
2 tablespoons baking cocoa

¼ teaspoon baking powder
¼ teaspoon salt
2 cups miniature marshmallows
1 cup (1 6-ounce package) semisweet chocolate chips
1 cup peanut butter
1½ cups crispy rice cereal

Preheat the oven to 350°F. In a large bowl, cream the butter and sugar with an electric mixer, then beat in the eggs and vanilla. In a separate bowl, combine the flour, pecans, cocoa, baking powder, and salt; add to the butter mixture, blending thoroughly. Spread the mixture into a greased 9" × 13" baking pan. Bake for 15 to 20 minutes or until a wooden toothpick inserted in the center comes out clean. Sprinkle the marshmallows evenly over the top and bake for 3 minutes more. Remove from the oven to cool. In a small saucepan, melt the chocolate chips and peanut butter together over low heat; remove from the heat and stir in the cereal. Spread the mixture over the cooled uncut bars. Chill, then cut into 3" × 6" bars. Keep refrigerated.

These Bars Are Stars

Fruit Bars

20 bars

Here's an old-time favorite that tastes like it came from Grandma's kitchen.

½ cup (1 stick) butter, softened
1 cup sugar
1 teaspoon vanilla extract
2 eggs, beaten
⅔ cup all-purpose flour

1 teaspoon baking powder
¼ teaspoon salt
1 cup chopped walnuts
1 cup chopped dates
½ cup candied cherries

Preheat the oven to 350°F. In a large bowl, cream the butter and sugar. Add the vanilla and eggs. In a medium-sized bowl, combine the flour, baking powder, and salt. Remove ½ cup of the flour mixture and combine it with the nuts, dates, and cherries; set aside. Slowly blend the remaining flour mixture into the butter mixture, mixing well. Stir in the fruit mixture. Pour the batter into a greased 8-inch square baking pan and bake for 45 minutes. Cool, then cut into bars.

These Bars Are Stars

Seven Layers of Heaven

about 2 dozen bars

Can't decide if you feel like chocolate . . . coconut . . . peanut butter or walnuts? Well, here's an easy way to make up your mind—have 'em all!

½ cup (1 stick) butter, melted
1 cup graham cracker crumbs
1 cup flaked coconut
1 cup (1 6-ounce package) semisweet chocolate chips

1 cup peanut butter chips
1 can (14 ounces) sweetened condensed milk
1 cup chopped walnuts

Preheat the oven to 350°F. Pour the melted butter evenly over the bottom of 9-inch square baking pan. Spread the graham cracker crumbs evenly over the butter. Then layer with the coconut, chocolate chips, then the peanut butter chips, one on top of the other in the order listed. Drizzle the sweetened condensed milk over the top layer and sprinkle with the walnuts. Bake for 30 minutes or until lightly browned. Cool, then cut into bars.

NOTE: Be sure to use sweetened condensed milk and not evaporated milk.

 Cookie Jar Favorite

These Bars Are Stars

Lemon Cheese Squares

24 squares

The tantalizing taste of lemon makes these truly irresistible! They're so light, they practically melt in your mouth.

1 package (18.25 ounces) yellow cake mix with pudding
2 eggs
⅓ cup vegetable oil

1 package (8 ounces) cream cheese, softened
⅓ cup sugar
1 teaspoon lemon juice

Preheat the oven to 350°F. In a medium-sized bowl, combine the cake mix, 1 egg, and the oil; mix until crumbly. Reserve 1 cup of the mixture. Lightly pat the remaining mixture into an ungreased 9" × 13" baking pan. Bake for 15 minutes. Meanwhile, in another medium-sized bowl, beat together the remaining egg, the cream cheese, sugar, and lemon juice until light and smooth. Spread over the baked layer. Sprinkle with the reserved crumb mixture and bake for another 15 minutes, until light golden. Cool, then cut into squares.

These Bars Are Stars

Double Chocolate Cookie Bars

16 bars

They say, "Twice is nice." See for yourselves, chocolate lovers!

2 cups crushed chocolate
   sandwich cookies
¼ cup (½ stick) butter,
   melted
2 cups (1 12-ounce package)
   semisweet chocolate
   chips, divided

1 can (14 ounces) sweetened
   condensed milk
1 teaspoon vanilla extract
1 cup chopped walnuts

Preheat the oven to 350°F. In a large bowl, combine the crushed cookies and butter; press the mixture onto the bottom of a 9" × 13" baking dish and set aside. In a medium-sized saucepan, combine 1 cup chocolate chips, the sweetened condensed milk, and the vanilla over medium heat; cook until the chips are melted, stirring frequently. Pour the mixture evenly over the prepared cookie crust. Top with the nuts and the remaining chocolate chips. Bake for 20 minutes or until set. Cool, then cut into bars.

NOTE: Don't be afraid to be adventurous and try different kinds of nuts.

These Bars Are Stars

Fudge Cheesecake Bars

36 bars

Rich fudge and creamy cheesecake? Say no more; the name speaks for itself.

4 bars (1 ounce each) Hershey's unsweetened baking chocolate
1 cup (2 sticks) butter
2½ cups sugar, divided
4 eggs
1 teaspoon vanilla extract

2 cups all-purpose flour
1 package (8 ounces) cream cheese, softened
1 package (13 ounces) Hershey's Hugs Chocolates or Hugs with Almonds chocolates, divided

Preheat the oven to 350°F. Place the baking chocolate and butter in a large microwaveable bowl. Microwave on high for 2 to 2½ minutes, stirring after each minute, until the chocolate and butter are completely melted. Beat in 2 cups sugar, 3 eggs, and the vanilla until blended. Stir in the flour, then spread the batter into a greased 9" × 13" baking pan. In a medium-sized bowl, beat the cream cheese, the remaining ½ cup sugar, and the remaining egg. Remove the wrappers from 12 chocolate pieces; coarsely chop, then stir them into the cream cheese mixture. Drop by dollops over the top of the chocolate batter. With a knife, swirl the chocolate batter to the top to create a marbled effect. Bake for 35 to 40 minutes or just until set. Cool completely in the pan on a wire rack. Cut into bars. Remove the wrappers from the remaining chocolate pieces and press them onto the tops of the bars. Cover and refrigerate any leftover bars.

NOTE: The time required to melt the chocolate and butter will depend on the wattage of your microwave. Check and stir mixture frequently, just until melted.

These Bars Are Stars

Strawberry Bars

3 dozen bars

These cakelike cookies bring the taste of springtime to any season.

1 cup (2 sticks) butter, softened	2 cups all-purpose flour
1/3 cup granulated sugar	1/2 cup strawberry jam
1 tablespoon sour cream	2 tablespoons light brown sugar
1 egg	1/4 cup chopped walnuts

Preheat the oven to 375°F. In a medium-sized bowl, beat the butter and granulated sugar until creamy. Beat in the sour cream and egg. Stir in the flour, 1/2 cup at a time, until a soft dough forms. Press 1 1/4 cups of the dough into the bottom of a 9-inch square baking pan that has been coated with nonstick vegetable cooking spray. Spread the jam evenly over the dough, then pat the remaining dough over the top. Sprinkle evenly with the brown sugar and the nuts. Bake for about 35 minutes. Remove from the oven and place the pan on a wire rack to cool completely. Cut into bars.

These Bars Are Stars

Golden Pecan Raisin Bars

20 bars

A nice change from all the rich chocolatey bars and cookies.

1 ¼ cups all-purpose flour
½ cup granulated sugar
½ cup (1 stick) butter,
   softened
2 eggs
½ cup firmly packed brown
   sugar

1 teaspoon vanilla extract
⅛ teaspoon baking soda
1 cup chopped pecans
1 cup golden raisins
½ cup flaked coconut

Preheat the oven to 350°F. In a medium-sized bowl, combine the flour and granulated sugar. Using a fork, cut in the butter until the mixture resembles fine meal. Press the mixture into a greased 8-inch square baking dish. Bake for 20 minutes or until the edges are golden. In a large bowl, beat together the eggs, brown sugar, and vanilla. Stir in the remaining ingredients. Evenly spread the batter over the warm crust and bake for an additional 20 to 25 minutes or until set. Cool pan on a wire rack and cut into bars when cool.

NOTE: We're going for a light look here, but if you don't have golden raisins, it's okay to use dark raisins instead.

These Bars Are Stars

Chocolate Diamonds

about 2 dozen

Here's a jewel of a cookie recipe to dazzle your family and friends.

1 square (1 ounce)
  unsweetened baking
  chocolate
¼ cup (½ stick) butter
½ cup sugar

1 egg
¼ cup all-purpose flour
⅛ teaspoon salt
¼ teaspoon vanilla extract
⅓ cup finely chopped walnuts

Preheat the oven to 400°F. In a medium-sized saucepan, melt the chocolate and butter over low heat. Remove from the heat and add all the remaining ingredients except the nuts. Spread the mixture into a greased 8-inch square baking pan. Sprinkle with the walnuts and bake for about 12 minutes. Cool slightly, then cut into 1¼-inch diamond shapes. Cool completely before removing from the pan.

NOTE: It's best not to substitute margarine for butter in this recipe.

These Bars Are Stars

Graham Cracker Bites

18 bars

The tastes from our childhood that we never outgrew . . .

2½ cups crushed graham
   crackers
1 can (14 ounces) sweetened
   condensed milk

2 eggs
1 cup (1 6-ounce package)
   semisweet chocolate chips
1 cup chopped walnuts

Preheat the oven to 350°F. In a large bowl, combine the graham crackers, sweetened condensed milk, and eggs. Add the chocolate chips and walnuts, mixing well. Pour into a 9" × 13" baking pan that has been coated with nonstick vegetable cooking spray. Bake for 30 minutes. Cut into 3" × 6" bars. Cool.

Chocolatey Date Fingers

2½ dozen bars

If your kids chew on these fingers, no one will mind!

1¼ cups chopped dates
¾ cup firmly packed brown sugar
½ cup (1 stick) butter
½ cup water
1 cup (1 6-ounce package) semisweet chocolate chips

1½ cups all-purpose flour
¾ teaspoon baking powder
½ teaspoon salt
2 eggs
1 cup orange juice
½ cup sliced almonds

Preheat the oven to 350°F. In a large saucepan, combine the dates, brown sugar, butter, and water. Cook, stirring occasionally, until a smooth paste forms. Remove from the heat. Stir in the chocolate chips while the mixture is hot. Let cool, then add the remaining ingredients. Spread the mixture evenly into a 10" × 15" rimmed cookie sheet that has been coated with nonstick vegetable cooking spray. Bake for 20 to 25 minutes. Cool on a wire rack and cut into 2" × 3" bars.

NOTE: You can find chopped dates in the supermarket produce department or with the baking supplies.

These Bars Are Stars

Brownies, Everyone's Favorites

How could I collect my favorite cookie recipes without including a chapter on brownies? Brownies are really bar cookies, but the special thing about them is how rich and mouth-watering they are.

Most people remember dark, chewy brownies from their childhood, but today there are so many different varieties that you could bake a different brownie every day for a year without repeating!

I had to choose a handful to include in this chapter, so these are a few of my very favorites. In a jiffy you can whip up a brownie as a snack or a fancy dessert. It's sure to bring smiles to the whole gang. Of course, don't forget the cold milk to go with them!

Before going on, why not check out the bar cookie tips on pages 159 and 160, since, after all, brownies are everyone's favorite bar cookies!

Brownies, Everyone's Favorites

Cookie Jar Favorites

Traditional Brownies

about 16 brownies

No matter what else you have for dessert, it seems that brownies are the biggest "seller." You'll sure know why when you try these chewy, bar-like brownies.

3 squares (1 ounce each) unsweetened baking chocolate
½ cup (1 stick) butter
1 cup sugar
2 eggs, beaten

⅔ cup all-purpose flour
Pinch of salt
1 teaspoon vanilla extract
1 cup chopped walnuts or other nuts (optional)

Preheat the oven to 350°F. In a double boiler or a saucepan, melt the chocolate and butter. Remove from heat and transfer to a large bowl. Beat in the sugar and eggs. Stir in the flour, salt, and vanilla until well blended. Stir in the nuts. Pour the batter into a greased 8-inch square baking pan and bake for 30 to 35 minutes, or until the top is dry and almost firm to the touch. Turn upside down on a wire rack and cool. Cut into squares.

NOTE: If you want to frost these, wait until they're cool.

Fudgy Brownies

about 30 brownies

These are the fudgy brownies that we all had as kids. (You remember how good they were, but do you remember them being this simple?)

1 cup (2 sticks) butter,
   melted
¾ cup baking cocoa
2 cups sugar
4 eggs
1 cup all-purpose flour
2 teaspoons vanilla extract

½ teaspoon salt
2 cups (1 12-ounce package)
   semisweet chocolate
   chunks
1 cup chopped nuts, your
   favorite type (optional)

Preheat the oven to 350°F. Place the melted butter into a large bowl; add the cocoa and stir until well blended. Add the sugar, mix well. Add the eggs, one at a time, beating well after each addition. Add the flour, vanilla, and salt; stir *just until combined*. Stir in the chocolate chunks and nuts. Spread the batter into a greased 9" × 13" baking pan; bake for about 40 minutes or until done. Cool and cut into serving-sized pieces.

NOTE: Sure, semisweet chocolate chips may be substituted for the chunks.

Butterscotch Brownies

about 2 dozen brownies

I've heard that some folks keep this recipe a secret from everyone but family. Well, I'll share mine!

2 eggs
½ cup all-purpose flour
¼ cup sugar
½ teaspoon baking powder
2 packages (4 ounces each)
    butterscotch pudding and
    pie filling mix

⅓ cup butter, melted
½ teaspoon vanilla extract
¼ cup chopped almonds
½ cup butterscotch chips

Preheat the oven to 325°F. In a large bowl, beat the eggs until very thick. Add all the remaining ingredients, mixing well. Pour the mixture into a lightly greased 9-inch square baking pan. Bake for 35 to 40 minutes or until a wooden toothpick inserted in the center comes out clean. Place pan on a wire rack to cool slightly, then cut into bars.

Brownies, Everyone's Favorites

Peanut Butter Cup Brownies

about 2 dozen brownies

A scrumptious combination that will get a standing ovation every time.

½ cup mayonnaise
2 eggs, beaten
¼ cup water
1 package (21.5 ounces)
   fudge brownie mix

1 bag (7 ounces) chocolate-
   covered peanut butter
   cups

Preheat the oven to 350°F. In a large bowl, combine the mayonnaise, eggs, and water until well blended. Stir in the brownie mix, mixing just until moistened. Coarsely chop the peanut butter cups and stir into the brownie mixture. Pour into a 9" × 13" baking pan that has been coated with nonstick vegetable cooking spray. Bake for 30 to 35 minutes or until the edges pull away from the sides of the pan.

NOTE: Don't chop the peanut butter cups too fine or you'll ruin the special treat in each bite.

Cookie Jar Favorite

Brownies, Everyone's Favorites

Disappearing Marshmallow Brownies

about 16 brownies

The marshmallows disappear during the baking, the brownies disappear right out of the oven—magic!!

½ cup vegetable shortening
2 squares (1 ounce each) unsweetened baking chocolate
2 eggs
1 cup sugar
1 cup all-purpose flour
¼ teaspoon baking powder

¼ teaspoon salt
3 tablespoons strong black coffee
1 teaspoon vanilla extract
1 cup miniature marshmallows
1 cup chopped walnuts

Preheat the oven to 350°F. Melt the shortening and chocolate in the top of a double boiler or in a saucepan over low heat; remove from heat. In a large bowl, beat the eggs. Add the sugar and chocolate mixture; beat for 1 minute. In a medium-sized bowl combine the flour, baking powder, and salt; blend into chocolate mixture. Add the coffee and vanilla, mixing well. Stir in the marshmallows and walnuts. Spread the batter into an 8-inch square baking dish that has been coated with nonstick vegetable cooking spray. Bake for 35 to 40 minutes. Cool, then cut into squares.

NOTE: The marshmallows melt and disappear during baking, leaving their flavor behind.

Brownies, Everyone's Favorites

Speckled Blonde Brownies

24 to 36 bars

Don't let the light color fool you . . . these brownies are heavy hitters.

⅔ cup vegetable shortening
2 cups light brown sugar
2 tablespoons hot water
2 eggs
2 tablespoons vanilla extract
2 cups all-purpose flour

1 teaspoon baking powder
¼ teaspoon baking soda
1 teaspoon salt
1 cup chopped walnuts
1 cup (1 6-ounce package)
	semisweet chocolate chips

Preheat the oven to 350°F. Melt the shortening in the microwave in a small microwaveable bowl (or on the stove in a small saucepan); let cool slightly. Transfer to a large bowl when cool, then add the brown sugar, hot water, eggs, and vanilla; blend well. Add the flour, baking powder, baking soda, and salt. Beat until thoroughly mixed. In a small bowl, combine the nuts and chocolate chips; reserve ½ cup of the combined nuts and chocolate chips and stir the rest into the batter, mixing evenly. Spread the batter evenly into a greased 9" × 13" baking dish. Sprinkle the top with the reserved ½ cup nut–chocolate chip combination. Bake for 25 to 30 minutes or until a wooden toothpick inserted in the center comes out clean.

NOTE: Have fun with this and try substituting either butterscotch or peanut butter chips for the chocolate chips. Mmm . . .

Brownies, Everyone's Favorites

Double Chocolate Mint Bars

32 bars

Awesome, absolutely awesome. Everyone I've shared these with (even nonmint lovers) has not been able to stop oohing and ahhing . . . well, maybe they have—just long enough to ask for more!

Chocolate Bottom

1 cup all-purpose flour
1 cup granulated sugar
½ cup (1 stick) butter

4 eggs
1½ cups (16 ounces)
   chocolate-flavored syrup

Mint Cream Layer

2 cups confectioners' sugar
½ cup (1 stick) butter,
   softened
1 tablespoon water

½ teaspoon mint extract
3 drops green food color

Chocolate Topping

6 tablespoons (¾ stick) butter

1 cup (1 6-ounce package)
   semisweet chocolate chips

Preheat the oven to 350°F. In a large bowl, combine the Chocolate Bottom ingredients and mix until smooth. Pour mixture into a greased 9" × 13" baking pan and bake for 25 to 30 minutes, or until a wooden toothpick inserted in the center comes out clean. Cool completely. In a large bowl, combine the Mint Cream Layer ingredients and beat

 Cookie Jar Favorite

Brownies, Everyone's Favorites

until smooth. Spread over the cooled bottom layer. Refrigerate for 1 hour. Place the Chocolate Topping ingredients in a small microwaveable bowl and melt on high power in the microwave. Stir with a wooden spoon until blended and smooth. Spread over the cooled mint cream layer. Refrigerate for 1 hour, then serve.

NOTE: These must be kept refrigerated or the top layers will melt. It's best not to substitute margarine for butter in this recipe.

Almond Brownies

about 28 brownies

Easy, easy, easy with the big flavor of almonds!

1 package (21.5 ounces) brownie mix
½ cup water
½ cup vegetable oil
1 egg

½ can (8 ounces) almond paste, formed into peanut-sized balls
½ cup slivered almonds

Preheat the oven to 350°F. In a large bowl, mix the brownie mix, water, oil, and egg until blended. Gently fold in the almond paste balls and nuts. Pour the batter evenly into a greased 9" × 13" baking pan. Bake for 33 to 35 minutes. *Do not overbake.* Cool completely, then cut.

NOTE: Almond paste has the texture of soft clay, so making the peanut-sized balls is easy—a fun job for the kids, too.

Brown Sugar Brownies

12 to 16 brownies

*It seems you can't go wrong with this recipe . . . I know, 'cause I've over-baked it **and** underbaked it. Here's what I found out: If you bake it a little less, it's chewy and delicious. If you bake it a little more, it's cakey and delicious. Now, **that's** an amazing recipe, hmm?!*

½ cup (1 stick) butter, softened to room temperature

2 cups firmly packed dark brown sugar

2 eggs, well beaten

1 cup all-purpose flour

1 teaspoon baking powder

1 teaspoon vanilla extract

1 cup pecan pieces

Confectioners' sugar for sprinkling (optional)

Preheat the oven to 350°F. In a large bowl, cream the softened butter; add the brown sugar and eggs. Mix thoroughly; add the flour and baking powder and blend. Stir in the vanilla and nuts. Pour the mixture into a well-greased 8-inch square baking pan and bake for 35 to 40 minutes. Cool in the pan, then cut into squares and sprinkle with confectioners' sugar, if desired.

 Cookie Jar Favorite

Chocolate Butterscotch Brownies

about 16 brownies

These go like hotcakes, so you just might want to whip up a double batch!

1½ cups all-purpose flour
2 teaspoons baking cocoa
1½ teaspoons baking powder
½ teaspoon salt
2 eggs

1 cup sugar
⅓ cup vegetable oil
1 teaspoon vanilla extract
2 cups (1 12-ounce package)
   butterscotch chips

Preheat the oven to 350°F. In a medium-sized bowl, mix the flour, cocoa, baking powder, and salt. In a large bowl, beat the eggs until foamy. Add the sugar, oil, and vanilla. Beat until well blended. Add the flour mixture, mixing well. Stir in the butterscotch chips. Pour the batter into a greased 8-inch square baking pan. Bake for about 30 minutes or until done. Cool, then cut into squares.

Brownies, Everyone's Favorites

Double Coffee Brownies

about 36 brownies

Want the fancy tastes of rich chocolate and ground roast coffee without any fuss? The whole gang will wonder when you had time.

1 cup all-purpose flour
½ teaspoon baking powder
¼ teaspoon salt
⅓ cup hot water
1 tablespoon instant
   granulated coffee

1 cup granulated sugar
½ cup (1 stick) butter
1 cup (1 6-ounce package)
   semisweet chocolate chips
3 eggs

Coffee Frosting

½ cup heavy cream
1 teaspoon instant granulated
   coffee

1 cup (1 6-ounce package)
   semisweet chocolate chips
½ cup confectioners' sugar

Preheat the oven to 350°F. In a small bowl, combine the flour, baking powder, and salt; set aside. In a medium-sized heavy saucepan, combine the hot water and 1 tablespoon instant coffee; heat to dissolve. Stir in the granulated sugar and butter; cook over low heat, stirring constantly, until the mixture comes to a boil. Remove from the heat; add 1 cup chocolate chips, stirring until smooth. Stir in the eggs one at a time, stirring well after each addition. Stir in the flour mixture. Pour into a greased 9-inch square baking pan. Bake for 25 to 30 minutes. Cool in the pan. Meanwhile, in a small, heavy saucepan, combine the cream and 1 teaspoon instant coffee; heat to dissolve.

Brownies, Everyone's Favorites

Add the remaining 1 cup chocolate chips and stir until smooth. Remove from the heat and stir in the confectioners' sugar. Chill until frosting reaches spreading consistency. Spread over the cooled brownies, then cut into 2¼-inch squares.

NOTE: You can use decaffeinated coffee or, for a stronger coffee flavor, substitute espresso powder or crystals for the regular instant coffee, if desired.

Brownies, Everyone's Favorites

Chocolate Rum Raisin Brownies

16 brownies

These are a special-occasion bittersweet chocolate brownie, so why not make any day a special occasion?

½ cup (1 stick) butter
3 squares (1 ounce each) unsweetened baking chocolate
1 cup sugar
2 eggs
2 teaspoons rum extract

1 cup all-purpose flour
1 cup rolled oats
½ teaspoon baking powder
½ teaspoon ground cinnamon
¼ teaspoon salt
½ cup raisins

Preheat the oven to 350°F. In a medium-sized saucepan, melt the butter and chocolate over low heat, stirring until smooth. Remove from the heat, scraping mixture into a large bowl; set aside for 10 minutes or until cool. With an electric mixer, beat the sugar, eggs, and rum extract into the chocolate mixture. In a medium-sized bowl, combine the flour, rolled oats, baking powder, cinnamon, and salt. Stir the flour mixture into the chocolate mixture until well blended. Fold in the raisins. Spread the batter evenly into a greased 9-inch square baking pan. Bake for 20 to 25 minutes or until a wooden toothpick inserted in the center comes out clean. Cut into 16 squares and let cool completely.

NOTE: If you prefer, you can substitute 2 tablespoons of dark rum for the 2 teaspoons of rum extract.

Pecan Pie Brownies

about 28 brownies

Is there anybody who doesn't like pecan pie? Is there anybody who doesn't like brownies? Put 'em together and **WOWEE!**

2 eggs
⅓ cup water
¼ cup vegetable oil
1 can (12.5 ounces) pecan
    filling

1 package (21.5 ounces)
    brownie mix
½ cup chopped pecans

Preheat the oven to 350°F. In a medium-sized bowl, mix the eggs, water, oil, and pecan filling until blended. Add the brownie mix and mix by hand until blended. Pour into a greased 9" × 13" baking pan. Sprinkle the chopped pecans on top. Bake for 33 to 35 minutes. Cool, then cut into squares.

NOTE: Pecan filling should be available either in the baking section or with the pie fillings in your favorite supermarket.

Double Chocolate Caramel Brownies

about 24 brownies

Rich, chewy, and irresistible . . .

I box (18.25 ounces) German
　or other chocolate
　cake mix
¾ cup (1½ sticks) butter,
　melted
⅔ cup evaporated milk,
　divided

I cup chopped pecans
2 packages (7 ounces each)
　chocolate-covered
　caramels
I cup (1 6-ounce package)
　semisweet chocolate chips

Preheat the oven to 350°F. In a large bowl, combine the cake mix, butter, ⅓ cup evaporated milk, and the pecans, stirring with a spoon until a dough forms. Press half the dough (2 cups) into a greased and floured 9" × 13" baking pan. Bake for 6 minutes. Meanwhile, in a medium-sized saucepan, over low heat, melt the caramels with the remaining ⅓ cup evaporated milk. Remove from the oven and pour the chocolate chips over the warm dough. Spread the melted caramels over the chips, then cover the top with the remaining dough. Bake for 20 minutes. Cool in the refrigerator for 30 minutes before cutting.

NOTE: If you prefer, you can use plain caramels rather than chocolate-covered ones.

Is It Cookie or Is It Candy?

How many times have you picked up a wonderful confection and asked yourself, "Is it a cookie or is it candy?" Well, put aside the store-bought gumdrops and chocolate bars, 'cause I've got some eyebrow raisers in this chapter!

They're sure great for entertaining, but they also make super afternoon "pick-me-ups." Why not get the whole family involved in making these creations? It'd be a great after-school or rainy day project for the kids.

Tips

- Try making candies in different shapes. It adds fun and variety to each recipe.

- Use waxed paper between layers of sticky candy to prevent candy from sticking together.

- Wrap candy tightly to keep it fresh. For a fancy look, bite-sized candy can be wrapped individually.

- Store chocolates in a cool location and out of direct sunlight.

- Try making three or four of your favorites, then make up candy tins or baskets to give as gifts, or just to let someone special know they're remembered. It's a gift everyone will love.

Is It Cookie or Is it Candy?

 Cookie Jar Favorites

Truffles

about 2½ dozen pieces

*These aren't the fancy truffles from France (those take **lots** more time), but these certainly will impress.*

½ cup undiluted evaporated milk

¼ cup sugar

2 cups (1 12-ounce package) semisweet chocolate chips

2 teaspoons instant coffee, dissolved in 1 tablespoon hot water

1 cup finely chopped toasted almonds

In a small heavy saucepan, combine the evaporated milk and sugar; cook over medium heat until mixture comes to a rolling boil. Boil for 3 minutes, stirring constantly. Remove from the heat. Stir in the chocolate chips and dissolved coffee until the chocolate is melted and the mixture is smooth. Chill for 1 hour. Shape into 1-inch balls, then roll in the almonds. Chill until ready to serve.

Peanut Clusters

3 to 4 dozen clusters

You can make these in a jiffy, but they'll think you got 'em in a candy store.

2 cups (1 12-ounce package) semisweet chocolate chips

1 cup sweetened condensed milk
2 cups salted peanuts

In a small saucepan, melt the chocolate chips over very low heat. Remove from the heat and stir in the sweetened condensed milk and peanuts. Drop by teaspoonfuls onto a cookie sheet that has been lined with waxed paper. Chill thoroughly before serving.

Is It Cookie or Is It Candy?

Rocky Road Fudge

9 to 10 dozen candies

For the chocolate lover, the fudge fanatic, and the insatiable sweet tooth—here's one that'll keep them all happy!

4 cups sugar
½ cup (1 stick) butter
1 can (12 ounces) evaporated milk
2 packages (12 ounces each) semisweet chocolate chips
1 jar (7½ ounces) marshmallow creme

2 teaspoons vanilla extract
2 cups miniature marshmallows
2 cups coarsely chopped salted peanuts

In a medium-sized saucepan, combine the sugar, butter, and evaporated milk, and cook over medium heat, stirring occasionally until the mixture comes to a full boil, 7 to 10 minutes. Boil, stirring constantly, until a candy thermometer reaches 228°F. or a small amount of the mixture dropped into ice water forms a 2-inch soft thread, 5 to 6 minutes. Remove from the heat; gradually stir in the chocolate chips until melted. Stir in the marshmallow creme until well blended. Stir in the vanilla. Stir in the marshmallows and peanuts, leaving a marbled effect. Spread the mixture into a lightly buttered 9" x 13" baking pan. Cover and refrigerate until completely cooled. Cut into 1-inch squares. Store, covered, in the refrigerator.

NOTE: For a softer fudge, store at room temperature.

It's best not to substitute margarine for butter in this recipe.

Turkish Sesame Treats

16 squares

An unusual sweet treat that tastes as exotic as it sounds.

½ cup (1 stick) butter
1 cup sesame seed
1¼ cups all-purpose flour
½ cup slivered almonds
1 tablespoon honey

1 can (14 ounces) sweetened
 condensed milk
½ cup whole milk
1 teaspoon vanilla extract

In a heavy skillet, melt the butter over medium heat. Add the sesame seed, stirring and cooking until golden brown, about 5 minutes. Add the flour and continue stirring until golden brown. Remove from the heat. Add the remaining ingredients and mix well. Cook over medium heat, stirring constantly, until the mixture is glossy and leaves the sides of the pan, about 3 minutes. Pat the mixture into a greased 8-inch square baking pan and refrigerate for at least 2 hours. Cut into 2-inch squares.

NOTE: It's best not to substitute margarine for butter in this recipe.

Peanut Butter Chocolate Candy Cookies

25 to 30 squares

It doesn't get any easier than this—you don't even have to turn on the oven! But you'll certainly turn on their appetites.

1 cup creamy peanut butter
1 cup (2 sticks) butter, melted
1 cup graham cracker crumbs

1 box (16 ounces) confectioners' sugar
2 cups (1 12-ounce package) semisweet chocolate chips, melted

In a large bowl, combine the peanut butter, melted butter, graham cracker crumbs, and confectioners' sugar; mix well with a wooden spoon. Press the mixture into a well-greased 10" x 15" rimmed cookie sheet. Pour the melted chocolate evenly over the top. Refrigerate for 15 minutes. Slice into squares, but leave in the pan. Refrigerate until well chilled. Serve cold.

Is It Cookie or Is It Candy?

Marvelous Macaroons

25 to 30 macaroons

*What else can I say? They **are** marvelous!*

2⅔ cups flaked coconut
⅔ cup sugar
¼ cup all-purpose flour
¼ teaspoon salt
4 egg whites

1 teaspoon almond extract
1 cup chopped almonds
Candied cherry halves
   (optional)

Preheat the oven to 325°F. In a medium-sized bowl, combine the coconut, sugar, flour, and salt. Mix in the egg whites and almond extract. Stir in the almonds and mix well. Drop by teaspoonfuls onto lightly greased cookie sheets. Garnish with the candied cherry halves, if desired. Bake for 20 to 25 minutes or until the cookie edges are golden brown. Remove immediately to wire racks to cool.

 Cookie Jar Favorite

English Toffee Bars

about 4 dozen bars

Temptation never tasted so good—a heavenly combination of cinnamon, chocolate, and pecans.

1 cup sugar	1 teaspoon ground cinnamon
1 cup (2 sticks) butter, softened	1 cup chopped pecans
1 egg, separated	1 cup (1 6-ounce package) semisweet or milk
1¾ cups all-purpose flour	chocolate chips

Preheat the oven to 275°F. In a small bowl, beat together the sugar and butter with an electric mixer at medium speed until well mixed, 1 to 2 minutes, scraping the bowl often. Add the egg yolk and continue beating until well mixed. Reduce the speed to low. Continue beating, gradually adding the flour and cinnamon, for 1 to 2 minutes longer, scraping the bowl frequently. Press the dough evenly onto the bottom of a 10" x 15" rimmed cookie sheet. In another small bowl, beat the egg white with a fork, then brush it over the top of the dough. Sprinkle with the pecans, patting them lightly into the dough. Bake for 40 to 50 minutes or until the edges are lightly browned. Remove from the oven and sprinkle with the chocolate chips; let stand for 3 minutes, then swirl the chips lightly with a knife. Cut into squares, triangles, or diamonds while still warm. Cool in the pan on a wire rack.

NOTE: It's best not to substitute margarine for butter in this recipe.

Panda Patties

about 4 dozen patties

This wise man say: "Try this! You won't believe it's made with Chinese noodles!"

2 cups (1 12-ounce package) semisweet chocolate chips

2 cups (1 12-ounce package) butterscotch chips

2 cups (12 ounces) peanuts

1 can (3 ounces) Chinese noodles (about 2 cups)

In a medium-sized saucepan, melt the chocolate and butterscotch chips over low heat. Remove from heat and stir in the nuts and noodles. Drop by teaspoonfuls onto a cookie sheet that has been lined with waxed paper. Refrigerate until hard, about 20 minutes. Remove from pan and store at room temperature.

Is It Cookie or Is It Candy?

Peanut Break-up

32 squares

A sure-fire way to "break" the ice at any gathering.

1 cup (2 sticks) butter,
  softened
½ teaspoon salt
1½ teaspoons vanilla extract
1 cup firmly packed brown
  sugar

1 teaspoon baking soda
2 cups all-purpose flour
1 cup (1 6-ounce package)
  semisweet chocolate chips
½ cup roasted peanuts,
  chopped

Preheat the oven to 375°F. In a large bowl, blend together the butter, salt, and vanilla. Add the brown sugar, baking soda, and flour; mix well. Stir in the chocolate chips. Press the mixture into a greased and floured 10" x 15" rimmed cookie sheet and sprinkle with the peanuts. Bake for 25 minutes. Cool and cut into squares (or just break into pieces).

Is It Cookie or Is It Candy?

Chocolate-Glazed Almond Bars

20 bars

Cookies? Candy? Who cares?! Either way, they're still **SUPER***!*

1 cup all-purpose flour
½ teaspoon ground cinnamon
½ cup (1 stick) butter, softened
½ cup firmly packed brown sugar

1 egg, separated
½ teaspoon almond extract
1 cup (1 6-ounce package) semisweet chocolate chips, melted
¼ cup toasted sliced almonds

Preheat the oven to 275°F. In a medium-sized bowl, combine the flour and cinnamon; set aside. In a large bowl, cream together the butter and brown sugar until light and fluffy. Beat in the egg yolk and almond extract. Gradually add the flour mixture and blend. Spread the mixture into a 9-inch square baking pan that has been coated with nonstick vegetable cooking spray. Lightly beat the egg white and brush it over the top. Bake on the center rack of the oven for 30 to 35 minutes or until lightly browned. Place the pan on a baking rack to cool. Spread the melted chocolate over the top and sprinkle with the sliced almonds. Chill until the chocolate hardens, then cut into diagonal bars.

NOTE: Try being extra fancy and substitute chopped cashews or macadamia nuts for the almonds.

 Cookie Jar Favorite

Is It Cookie or Is It Candy?

Praline Squares

about 48 squares

Now wherever we are we can enjoy the taste of this Southern specialty.

24 whole graham crackers
1 cup (2 sticks) butter
1 cup firmly packed brown
   sugar

1 cup chopped pecans or
   walnuts

Preheat the oven to 350°F. Arrange the crackers 1 layer deep on an ungreased 10" × 15" rimmed cookie sheet. In a small saucepan, combine the butter and brown sugar; bring to a boil, stirring constantly, for 2 minutes. Stir in the nuts and mix well. Spoon the mixture over the graham crackers. Bake for 10 minutes. Remove from the oven and let stand for 2 minutes. Cut into squares while still warm. Store in tins or coffee cans.

NOTE: These taste just like Southern pralines, but they're so much easier to make!

   It's best not to substitute margarine for butter in this recipe.

Is It Cookie or Is It Candy?

Peanut Butterscotch Pretzel Snacks

60 pretzels

Some call it a snack, others a candy, while some insist it's a cookie. While they're deciding, I'm just eating 'em up.

2 cups (1 12-ounce package)
    butterscotch chips
⅓ cup peanut butter

60 3-inch twisted pretzels
2 to 3 tablespoons toasted
    sesame seed

In a medium-sized heavy saucepan over very low heat, melt the chips with the peanut butter, stirring until smooth. Remove from the heat. Dip about three-fourths of each pretzel in the peanut butter mixture; shake each pretzel, and scrape off the excess coating onto the edge of the pan. Place on a wire rack, then sprinkle lightly with sesame seed. Repeat with the remaining pretzels. (If the mixture thickens, warm it again over very low heat, stirring constantly.) Chill pretzels for 20 minutes or until set. Store in an airtight container or in plastic bags.

NOTE: You can use pretzels with no or low salt if you're watching your salt intake . . . and they're still just as yummy.

Brickle Crunch

25 to 30 servings

Folks are always impressed when we serve homemade candy 'cause they think it's so hard to make. (But we know the truth!)

35 saltine crackers (about 1 sleeve from a 16-ounce box)
1 cup (2 sticks) butter

1 cup sugar
1 cup (1 6-ounce package) semisweet chocolate chips
1 cup peanut butter chips

Preheat the oven to 400°F. Line a 10" x 15" rimmed cookie sheet with aluminum foil. Lay out the crackers on the cookie sheet, packing tightly. In a medium-sized saucepan, melt the butter, then add the sugar and boil, stirring frequently, for 2 to 3 minutes, until the sugar is completely dissolved. Immediately pour the mixture over the crackers and bake for 7 minutes. Remove from the oven and immediately sprinkle the chocolate and peanut butter chips over the crackers, spreading evenly as they melt. Refrigerate for at least 30 minutes, then break into pieces. Serve immediately or refrigerate until ready to serve.

NOTE: This is great topped with chopped nuts or flaked coconut; just sprinkle either on top before refrigerating.

It's best not to substitute margarine for butter in this recipe.

Chocolate Pecan Creams

about 3 dozen candies

So rich and nutty, you'll love taking the credit for these.

2 squares (1 ounce each)
   unsweetened baking
   chocolate
1 can (14 ounces) sweetened
   condensed milk

½ teaspoon vanilla extract
1½ cups chopped pecans

In the top of a double boiler or in a stainless steel bowl set over a saucepan of simmering water, heat the chocolate and sweetened condensed milk until the chocolate melts. Using an electric mixer, beat until the mixture thickens. Add the vanilla and stir well. Allow to cool long enough so that the mixture can be handled. Drop by teaspoonfuls into a bowl of chopped pecans. Form into 1-inch balls and place on a cookie sheet that has been lined with waxed paper. Chill in the refrigerator until firm.

NOTE: Make sure the chocolate mixture is cool enough to handle, but not too firm.

A Little Bit of This, A Little Bit of That

This has to be one of my favorite chapters in this book. It's a combination of all the goodies that don't really fit into the basic categories of cookie baking. Many of these recipes are favorites we've grown up with that can now easily be made at home. The rules are simple: Follow the recipe as written, and add your own touches. That's it!

This is the chapter where you can really be creative. Go for adding your favorite tastes to the recipes. Maybe try a different flavor liqueur in the Chocolate Chip Dome . . . or how 'bout an old-fashioned ice cream sandwich with your favorite **two** flavors of ice cream? There are no limits! Just have fun!

A Little Bit of This, A Little Bit of That

Cookie Jar Favorites

South of the Border Doughnuts

3 to 3½ dozen doughnuts

These Mexican treats are perfect for an after-siesta (or anytime) nibble.

⅔ cup sugar, divided
1 teaspoon ground cinnamon
¼ cup (½ stick) butter, softened
2 eggs
1 teaspoon vanilla extract

1¾ cups all-purpose flour, divided (more as needed)
2 teaspoons baking powder
1 teaspoon salt
¼ cup milk
Vegetable oil for frying

In a shallow pan, combine ⅓ sugar and the cinnamon; set aside. In a medium-sized bowl, using an electric mixer, cream together the butter and sugar until creamy. Add the eggs and vanilla, blending well. Mix in 1 cup of the flour, the baking powder, and salt; mix well and blend in the milk. Add the remaining flour and mix to make a soft dough. Turn out onto a floured surface and knead for 1 or 2 minutes until the dough is smooth, kneading in more flour if the dough is still too sticky to handle. With a rolling pin, roll out the dough to a ¼-inch thickness, flouring the surface and rolling pin lightly if the dough sticks. Cut the dough with a 2-inch round cookie cutter. In a heavy skillet or Dutch oven, heat 2 inches of oil over medium heat, until hot but not burning or smoking (350°F.). Fry six 2-inch rounds at a time, turning often with tongs, until puffy and golden, 1½ to 2 minutes. Drain on paper towels and toss in coating mix while still hot.

NOTE: These should look like puffy fried dough balls.

A Little Bit of This, A Little Bit of That

Dipped Apricots

20 to 24 pieces

Add a touch of elegance to holiday cookie and candy trays. Your guests will say, "Ooh very fancy!!"

1 package (7 ounces) chocolate caramel candies (about 1 cup)	2 packages (6 ounces each) large dried apricots
¼ cup heavy cream or evaporated milk	½ cup finely chopped toasted almonds

In a small heavy saucepan, heat the candies and cream over low heat, stirring frequently, until melted. Carefully dip two-thirds of each apricot in the melted chocolate, then in the nuts. Place the apricots in a single layer on a cookie sheet that has been lined with waxed paper. Chill until the chocolate is firm. Store in the refrigerator in an airtight container in layers separated by waxed paper.

NOTE: Twelve ounces of dried peaches will work well, too.

A Little Bit of This, A Little Bit of That

Black & Whites

3 to 3½ dozen cookies

These are favorites of families all over the United States—and everywhere I go I hear different names for them. The most common are Black & Whites and Halfmoons. (Whatever they're called, we all still love 'em!)

½ cup vegetable shortening
1 cup sugar
2 eggs
2 cups all-purpose flour
½ teaspoon baking powder
1 teaspoon vanilla extract
2 squares (1 ounce each)
 unsweetened baking
 chocolate, melted

1 cup (1 6-ounce package)
 chocolate chips, melted
½ cup milk
8 ounces (½ of a 16-ounce
 can) chocolate frosting
8 ounces (½ of a 16-ounce
 can) vanilla frosting

Preheat the oven to 350°F. In a large bowl, cream the shortening and sugar until light and creamy; beat in the eggs. Add the flour, baking powder, and vanilla, blending well. Stir in all of the melted chocolate and the milk, mixing well. Drop by heaping teaspoonfuls onto cookie sheets that have been coated with nonstick vegetable cooking spray. Bake for 7 to 10 minutes. Remove to wire racks to cool. Frost the flat side of each cookie, one half with vanilla frosting and the other half with the chocolate frosting.

NOTE: The leftover icing will keep in the refrigerator for weeks.

 Cookie Jar Favorite

Chocolate Chip Dome

12 to 16 servings

No one will ever be able to guess that the main ingredient in this awesome dessert is . . . store-bought chocolate chip cookies!

1½ cups milk
¾ cup coffee-flavored liqueur
1 package (18 ounces)
    chocolate chip cookies

1 container (16 ounces)
    frozen whipped topping,
    thawed

In a medium-sized bowl, combine the milk and liqueur. Dip the chocolate chip cookies in the milk mixture until moist, then use to completely line a 2-quart stainless-steel mixing bowl. Cover the cookies with a ½-inch layer of the whipped topping. Repeat layer after layer until all the cookies are used, reserving ¼ container of the whipped topping. Cover the bowl and freeze overnight. Remove from the freezer 1 hour before serving. Unmold by dipping the bowl in a warm water bath, making sure no water gets into the bowl. Turn out onto a serving platter and cover with the remaining whipped topping. Cut into pie-shaped servings.

NOTE: Soak the chocolate chip cookies until they are soft but not falling apart.

A Little Bit of This, A Little Bit of That

Pita Wedges

about 10 dozen

If you need to bake up a quick treat, you won't find anything faster than this.

1 package (12 ounces) pita breads	¼ cup confectioners' sugar plus extra for topping
½ cup (1 stick) butter, melted	1 teaspoon ground cinnamon

Preheat the oven to 400°F. Cut each pita bread in half horizontally, forming 2 rounds. Using a pastry brush, brush the rough sides of the pita breads with the melted butter. In a small bowl, combine the confectioners' sugar and cinnamon; sprinkle the mixture over the pita rounds by pouring it through a strainer. Cut each round into 4 strips, then cut each strip into 1½-inch pieces. Place on ungreased cookie sheets and bake until golden, about 5 minutes. Remove from the pan and cool on wire racks. Just before serving, sprinkle with additional confectioners' sugar. Store in airtight containers.

A Little Bit of This, A Little Bit of That

Old-Fashioned Ice Cream Sandwiches

about 15 sandwiches

Bet you never knew it was so effortless to make these at home. You probably already have everything you need . . . so go ahead and surprise them!

2 cups all-purpose flour
½ teaspoon salt
¾ cup sugar
⅓ cup baking cocoa
¾ cup (1½ sticks) butter,
    softened

1 egg
1 teaspoon vanilla extract
1 pint vanilla ice cream

In a large bowl, combine all the ingredients except the ice cream, blending well. Divide the dough in half and shape into two 3-inch-diameter rolls. Wrap in waxed paper and chill for 2 hours or overnight. Preheat the oven to 350°F. Unwrap the roll and cut into ⅛-inch-thick slices. Bake on ungreased cookie sheets for 8 to 10 minutes or until set. Cool slightly, loosen from pans (with a spatula), then allow to cool completely. Top 1 cookie at a time with a scoop of vanilla ice cream and top with a second cookie, pressing firmly to evenly spread the ice cream. Repeat until all the cookies are used. Freeze until set, then wrap each sandwich separately in plastic wrap.

NOTE: Try your favorite flavor ice cream. My personal favorite is mint chocolate chip.

A Little Bit of This, A Little Bit of That

Cookies in a Crust

6 to 8 servings

With this dessert nobody will have to decide between cookies and pie—they can have both!

2 eggs
⅓ cup all-purpose flour
⅓ cup granulated sugar
⅓ cup firmly packed brown
    sugar
½ cup (1 stick) butter,
    melted and cooled to
    room temperature

1 cup (1 6-ounce package)
    semisweet chocolate chips
⅔ cup chopped walnuts
1 prepared 9-inch butter-
    flavored pie crust

Preheat the oven to 325°F. In a large bowl, beat the eggs until foamy. Mix in the flour and sugars and blend well. Blend in the melted butter, then add the chocolate chips and walnuts. Pour the mixture into the pie crust and bake for about 1 hour.

A Little Bit of This, A Little Bit of That

Long-Stemmed Chocolate Chip Cookies

20 cookies

What better way to say "I love you" than with long-stemmed chocolate chip cookies?

½ cup vegetable shortening
½ cup granulated sugar
¼ cup firmly packed brown sugar
1 egg
1 teaspoon vanilla extract
1 cup all-purpose flour
½ teaspoon salt

½ teaspoon baking soda
1 cup (1 6-ounce package) semisweet chocolate chips
½ cup chopped walnuts
20 wooden skewers or popsicle sticks, 6 to 8 inches long

Preheat the oven to 375°F. In a medium-sized bowl, cream the shortening, sugars, egg, and vanilla until light. In another medium-sized bowl, combine the flour, salt, and baking soda. Add to the shortening mixture and blend well. Add the chocolate chips and nuts and stir until well mixed. Lay the skewers on cookie sheets that have been coated with nonstick vegetable cooking spray (7 or 8 per sheet). Spoon 1 tablespoon of the dough onto the end of each skewer, covering the top 2 inches of each skewer. Bake for 10 to 12 minutes or until golden. Let cool for 3 or 4 minutes and use a spatula to carefully remove the stemmed cookies to a wire rack to cool completely.

NOTE: Wrap a dozen long-stemmed chocolate chip cookies in waxed paper, plastic wrap, or tissue paper and tie with a ribbon to resemble a dozen long-stemmed roses . . . *wink, wink*.

A Little Bit of This, A Little Bit of That

Soft Chocolate Marshmallow Sandwiches

about 20 sandwiches

You had these devilishly good store-bought treats growing up, but once you make them yourself you'll never switch back.

½ cup vegetable shortening
1 cup granulated sugar
1 egg
½ cup baking cocoa
2 cups all-purpose flour

1 ½ teaspoons baking soda
½ teaspoon salt
1 cup milk
1 teaspoon vanilla extract

Filling

¾ cup (1 ½ sticks) butter, softened
1 ⅓ cups confectioners' sugar

1 cup marshmallow creme (about ½ of a 7½-ounce jar)
½ teaspoon vanilla extract

Preheat the oven to 400°F. In a large bowl, cream the shortening, granulated sugar, and egg until creamy. Add the cocoa. In a large bowl, combine the flour, baking soda, and salt. Add to the shortening mixture, alternately with the milk and vanilla. Drop by teaspoonfuls onto ungreased cookie sheets. Bake for 8 to 10 minutes. While baking, combine the filling ingredients in a medium-sized bowl and beat until smooth and creamy. Remove the cookies to wire racks. Frost the flat side of half of the cookies with the filling and put the remaining cookies on top, making sandwiches. Refrigerate to firm up the filling.

NOTE: When dropping the dough, flatten it lightly to get a wider, thinner cookie 'cause they rise while baking.

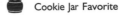 Cookie Jar Favorite

231

Cookie Pie Crust

one 6- to 8-serving pie crust

Everyone will ask you for the recipe for your fancy crust. It's okay to share this one with really good friends. Some suggested fillings are ice cream, pudding, mousse, canned pie filling, no-bake cheesecake (see **MR. FOOD**® *Makes Dessert, pages 58 and 59), or strawberry cream pie filling (***MR. FOOD**® *Makes Dessert, page 51).*

1½ cups cookie crumbs made from crisp cookies, such as butter cookies, vanilla and chocolate sandwich cookies, graham crackers, spice cookies, vanilla wafers, ginger snaps, or chocolate chip cookies

¼ cup (½ stick) butter, melted

Preheat the oven to 350°F. Crush your favorite cookies by rolling them in a plastic bag with a rolling pin, or in a food processor with a cutting blade, until a fine crumb mixture is formed. Place the crumbs in a medium-sized bowl and mix with the butter, blending well. Press into the bottom and sides of an 8- or 9-inch pie pan that has been coated with nonstick vegetable cooking spray. Bake for 8 to 10 minutes, then cool. Fill with your favorite filling and refrigerate or freeze as the filling requires.

NOTE: You can add several tablespoons of sugar to the cookie crumbs if a sweeter crust is desired.

Chocolate-Dipped Fruit

Everyone loves fresh fruit, and everyone loves chocolate. So, what could delight more than this spectacular combination?! (And it's as much fun to make as it is to eat!)

2 cups (1 12-ounce package) semisweet chocolate chips

Your favorite fruits (see below)

Melt (don't overheat) the chocolate chips any of these ways:

- In the top of a double boiler (over simmering water) over low heat, stirring occasionally

- In a stainless steel bowl over a saucepan of simmering water

- In the microwave in a microwaveable container (on medium or high power for 1 to 3 minutes)

When the chocolate is melted, remove it from the heat and dip your choice of fruit into it. (To keep it neat, you can insert a skewer or fork into the end of the fruit to dip it.) Shake any excess chocolate back into the pan and place the dipped fruit in a single layer on a waxed paper-lined cookie sheet until the chocolate firms up.
Here are some tips to help with your creations:

- Always clean and pat fruit completely dry before dipping it in the chocolate.

- Cut fruit into bite-sized pieces before dipping.

A Little Bit of This, A Little Bit of That

- Fruits that darken when exposed to air (bananas, apples, peaches, etc.) are best if completely coated with chocolate.

- Strawberries, apricots, and dried or candied fruits work well coated just halfway with chocolate.

- Fruit that is totally coated should be refrigerated; half-dipped fruit should be left at room temperature and used within eight to twelve hours.

NOTE: Be careful not to allow any water to mix with the chocolate because it will become grainy and will tighten up. If this happens, add 1 teaspoon of vegetable shortening to the chocolate and allow it to melt before continuing to dip fruit.

To Wash It All Down

Cookies, brownies, bars, and candy. So many goodies to choose from! Now that you've sampled the best of the best, you'll need a special beverage to wash it all down.

Here's a chapter full of just the right ones. There are hot drinks, cold drinks, and some that can be served either hot or cold!

I've started off with the crowd-pleasing punch bowl fillers, then I've narrowed it down to the drinks you can cuddle up with when you're home all by yourself. **ENJOY!!**

Tips

- For chilled drinks, chill the glasses, as well as all ingredients, before mixing.

- For punch bowl recipes, chill the punch bowl in advance, if possible. Also, make an ice ring by pouring water or fruit juice into a round gelatin mold. Try adding cherries and cut citrus fruit to the ring, too, for a fancy look. Freeze it, then add it to the punch instead of ice cubes. It'll keep the punch cold longer and, since it takes longer to melt, it won't water down the taste as quickly. To unmold, dip the mold in warm (not hot) water and invert mold carefully into the punch bowl; it should slip out easily. (Use chilled boiled water, rather than plain tap water, to make clearer ice molds.)

- Try making ice cubes from fruit juices or drink mixtures. Use instead of regular ice cubes for a different touch.

- Always serve ice cream and blender drinks immediately after making, to ensure the proper consistency.

- Use low heat when making hot milk and chocolate drinks, since both tend to scorch easily.

- Stirring hot milk drinks frequently prevents a "skin" from forming on the top.

- When adding milk or half-and-half to hot liquids, always add it gradually, while stirring.

To Wash It All Down

Creamy Maple Coffee Punch

12 to 15 servings

Iced coffee with a hint of maple sounds different, huh? Well, the taste will bring lots of oohs and ahhs (and without all the sugar of traditional iced coffee).

8 cups hot water
½ cup instant coffee
2 tablespoons vanilla extract

2 cups maple syrup
2 cups heavy cream
Ice cubes

In a large pot, bring the water to a boil and add the coffee, vanilla, and maple syrup. Let cool slightly, then refrigerate overnight. Stir in the cream. Serve in a punch bowl with lots of ice.

NOTE: Imitation maple syrup or pancake syrup will work fine, but for a true maple flavor, pure maple syrup is the best.

To Wash It All Down

Sparkling Garden Punch

12 servings

Not too tart, not too sweet . . . a combination of flavors they'll ask for again and again . . . and again!

1 can (12 ounces) frozen orange juice concentrate, thawed

1 can (12 ounces) frozen cranberry juice concentrate, thawed

1 can (12 ounces) frozen lemonade concentrate, thawed

4 cups cold water

1 bottle (33.8 ounces) ginger ale

In a punch bowl, combine all the ingredients except the ginger ale. Shortly before serving, add the ginger ale and some ice.

NOTE: Heat the leftover diluted punch in a saucepan and you'll have an elegant hot fruit drink.

239

To Wash It All Down

Old-Fashioned Hot Cocoa

12 servings

Wanna bring smiles to your whole gang, and warm their tummies, too?

¾ cup cocoa powder
¾ cup sugar
½ teaspoon salt

4 cups warm water
8 cups half-and-half
48 miniature marshmallows

In a large saucepan, combine the cocoa powder, sugar, and salt. Gradually stir in the water and simmer over low heat for 6 to 8 minutes, stirring occasionally. Gradually add the half-and-half and heat, but do not allow the mixture to boil. Remove from the heat. Serve in mugs, topped with the mini-marshmallows.

NOTE: You may substitute skim milk for the half-and-half if you want to cut down on the fat in this drink.

To Wash It All Down

Citrus Tea

8 servings

Most folks say that tea should be served in a teacup, but this tea should be served in a warmed mug to give you a warm, cozy feeling . . . try it, you'll see.

1 cup orange juice	1 lemon
6 cups water	⅓ cup honey
6 tea bags	⅓ cup sugar

In a large saucepan, combine the orange juice and water and bring to a boil. Dunk the tea bags in the water mixture and simmer for 5 minutes. Remove the tea bags and discard. Cut the lemon in half and squeeze its juice into the tea mixture, then place the lemon halves into the mixture. Stir in the honey and sugar. Serve immediately.

NOTE: If you prefer a sweeter tea, add more honey or sugar, as desired.

Steaming Mocha Cocoa

8 servings

Wanna make a real crowd-pleasing drink to wash down your favorite cookies, pies, or just about anything? Try this one.

6 cups water
1½ cups instant hot
    chocolate mix
3 tablespoons instant coffee

2 cups half-and-half
Aerosol whipped cream
    (optional)

In a large saucepan, bring the water to a boil; remove from heat. Gradually stir in the hot chocolate mix and the instant coffee until both are completely dissolved. Slowly add the half-and-half and stir until evenly mixed. Ladle into mugs and top with whipped cream, if desired.

NOTE: If you want a richer drink, you may substitute 2 cups heavy cream for the half-and-half.

Cranberry Refresher

6 servings

If you thought cranberries were just for the holidays, think again. This one's a year-'round winner, perfect to wash down anything, hot or cold.

1 can (16 ounces) jellied cranberry sauce
1 cup water
2 cups unsweetened pineapple juice

⅓ cup light brown sugar
8 ice cubes

Place all ingredients except the ice cubes in a blender and blend until smooth and frothy. Add the ice cubes and blend again until the ice is crushed. Serve immediately.

NOTE: This is just as good served warm, too. It makes a great steaming harvest drink or holiday specialty. Just replace the 8 ice cubes with an additional ¼ cup water, heat in a saucepan, and enjoy.

To Wash It All Down

Tropical Froth

6 servings

A drink so refreshing you can almost feel an exotic tropical breeze with each sip . . . really!

I can (6 ounces) frozen
   limeade concentrate,
   thawed
I can (6 ounces) pineapple
   juice
I bottle (33.8 ounces) ginger
   ale

2 cups rainbow sherbet
8 ice cubes
2 lemons, sliced

In a large punch bowl, combine the limeade, pineapple juice, and ginger ale. Add the sherbet and ice cubes just before serving. Garnish with the sliced lemons.

NOTE: If you don't have rainbow sherbet on hand, try substituting vanilla ice cream.

Spicy Apple Cider

5 to 6 servings

Nothing says "fall" like the taste of apple cider, and with the addition of a few special spices, it's now a drink that's a winner all year long.

1 quart apple cider
½ cup sugar
¼ teaspoon ground cloves

¼ teaspoon ground allspice
¼ teaspoon ground cinnamon

In a medium-sized saucepan, combine all the ingredients and bring to a boil. Reduce the heat and simmer for 15 minutes. Serve hot in mugs.

NOTE: This drink is great with Cheesy Wafers (page 100) for the all-American taste of apple pie and Cheddar cheese.

245

Icy Homemade Lemonade

6 servings

A down-home thirst-quencher that's as easy as 1, 2, 3!

6 cups cold water
4 to 5 fresh lemons
    (depending on size)

1 cup granulated sugar
10 ice cubes

Pour the cold water into a gallon jar or a large pitcher. Cut each lemon in half, squeeze the juice into the water, and add the lemon halves. Gradually add the sugar and stir until dissolved. Add the ice and serve.

NOTE: I like to use extra-fine granulated sugar in place of regular granulated sugar because it dissolves quicker. And you could simply make limeade by substituting 6 to 7 limes in place of lemons.

To Wash It All Down

Fuzzy Navel Froth

5 to 6 Servings

If you like creamsicles and you like peaches, well, I just found the perfect drink for you! Try dunking our Zesty Honey Crisps (page 96) in this for an after-school treat that will bring lots of smiles.

2 cups cold milk
2 cups cold orange juice

1 can (16 ounces) sliced peaches

In a blender, combine all ingredients and blend on high speed until peaches are puréed and frothy. Serve ice cold.

NOTE: I suggest refrigerating the peaches in advance to ensure an ice cold drink.

To Wash It All Down

Fancy Nonalcoholic Strawberry Daiquiri

4 servings

Thought you could only get those fancy drinks in fancy restaurants? Well, here's a recipe to make them feel special at home, too.

1½ cups whole or 2 percent milk

2 cups frozen strawberries, slightly thawed

2 scoops vanilla ice cream

2 teaspoons extra-fine granulated sugar

8 ice cubes

Combine all ingredients in a blender and blend until frothy.

NOTE: If you'd like, garnish each glass with a fresh strawberry or maybe a sprig of fresh mint, if available.

New York Egg Cream

1 to 2 servings

A traditional, refreshing favorite from the Lower East Side of New York that's certain to become a favorite in your house now, too.

3 tablespoons chocolate-
    flavored syrup
¾ cup cold club soda or
    seltzer water

¾ cup cold milk

Pour the chocolate-flavored syrup into a large glass, then add the club soda and stir just until mixed. Add the milk and stir just to combine. Serve ice cold.

NOTE: For a real sparkling treat, make sure the club soda or seltzer water has plenty of carbonation.

To Wash It All Down

Honey Nog

1 serving

Here's a quick drink to wash down all your favorite cookies, a taste you'll want to keep all to yourself.

1¼ cups ice cold whole milk   Pinch of ground nutmeg
2 tablespoons honey   1 teaspoon sugar
Pinch of ground cinnamon

Pour the milk into a chilled 12-ounce glass and stir in the honey. Combine the remaining ingredients in small bowl, then add to the milk and honey combination. Stir well and enjoy immediately.

NOTE: Mix up a double batch and share it with a friend.

Root Beer Float

I serving

Have a craving for a drink that brings back fond memories and delivers lots of lip-smackin' goodness? Try this to satisfy that craving.

¼ cup cold milk
2 scoops vanilla ice cream,
    divided

¾ cup chilled root beer soda

Pour the milk into a 12-ounce glass and add one scoop of ice cream. Stir in half of the root beer, then add the remaining scoop of ice cream and top with the remaining root beer.

NOTE: Make sure you use a straw and a long-handled spoon to help you enjoy every last bit. (It gives that old-fashioned ice cream fountain look, too!)

251

INDEX

254

Index

Index

Index

Let MR. FOOD® Take You On Exciting Food Adventures!

He's got *EASY* ideas for

**family dinners   soups and salads   pot luck dishes
barbecues   special brunches   unbelievable desserts**

...and that's just the beginning!

From New England Clam Chowder in *MR. FOOD® Cooks Real American*, Spaghetti Pie in *MR. FOOD® Cooks Pasta*, Garlic Roasted Potatoes in *MR. FOOD® Cooks Like Mama*, Friday Night Roasted Chicken in *The MR. FOOD® Cookbook, OOH it's so GOOD!!* ™, to Candy Apple Pie in *MR. FOOD® Makes Dessert* and Incredible Chocolate Chunks in *MR. FOOD®'s Favorite Cookies*, these **quick, no-fuss** recipes are just what you need to help make your life easier. So, don't miss out! Join in on the fun! It's so simple to share in all the
OOH it's so GOOD!!™

✂--

TITLE	PRICE		QUANTITY		
A. **MR. FOOD®** Cooks Like Mama	@ $12.95 ea.	x	_____	=	$_____
B. The **MR. FOOD®** Cookbook, OOH it's so GOOD!!™	@ $12.95 ea.	x	_____	=	$_____
C. **MR. FOOD®** Cooks Chicken	@ $ 9.95 ea.	x	_____	=	$_____
D. **MR. FOOD®** Cooks Pasta	@ $ 9.95 ea.	x	_____	=	$_____
E. **MR. FOOD®** Makes Dessert	@ $ 9.95 ea.	x	_____	=	$_____
F. **MR. FOOD®** Cooks Real American	@ $13.95 ea.	x	_____	=	$_____
G. **MR. FOOD®**'s Favorite Cookies	@ $11.95 ea.	x	_____	=	$_____

Book Total $_____

Send payment to: **MR. FOOD®**
P.O. Box 696
Holmes, PA 19043

+$2.95 Postage & Handling *First Copy* **AND**
$1 Ea. Add'l. Copy (Canadian Orders Add Add'l. $2.00 *Per Copy***)** $_____

Name_____

Subtotal $_____

Street_____

City_____State_____Zip_____

Less $1.00 per book if ordering 3 or more books with this order $-_____

Method of Payment: ☐Check or Money Order Enclosed
☐ Credit Card: ☐ Visa ☐ MasterCard Expiration Date_____

Add Applicable Sales Tax (FL Residents Only) $_____

Signature_____

Total in U.S. Funds $_____

Account # ☐☐☐☐☐☐☐☐☐☐☐☐☐☐☐☐

Please allow 6 to 8 weeks for delivery.   BKG1